Greening the Global Economy

March 2016
To Susant Cameron,

Greening the Global Economy

In solidary with
all of your important
contributions,

Robert Pollin   With best
wishes

Bob Poll.

A Boston Review Book
The MIT Press
Cambridge, Massachusetts
London, England

MIT Press books may be purchased at special quantity discounts for business or sales promotional use. For information, please email special_sales@mitpress.mit.edu.

This book was set in Stone by *Boston Review* and printed and bound in the United States of America.

Library of Congress Control Number: 2015953018
ISBN 978-0-262-02823-3 (hc. : alk paper)

10   9   8   7   6   5   4   3   2   1

For Judy Fogg, Jerry Epstein, and Jim Boyce

wonderful PERI co-workers; tremendous friends

Contents

1 Introduction: The Global Green Energy Challenge   1

2 Prospects for Fossil Fuels and Nuclear Power   21

3 Prospects for Energy Efficiency   31

4 Prospects for Clean Renewable Energy   45

5 How to Hit the CO_2 Emissions Reduction Target   62

6 Expanding Job Opportunities
through Clean Energy Investments   73

7 A Policy Agenda That Can Work   92

8 Risk, Ethics, and the Politics of Climate Stabilization   110

Appendix 1: Estimating Global Costs for
Expanding Clean Renewable Energy Productive Capacity   122

Appendix 2: Model for Estimating Global CO_2 Reductions
through 20-Year Clean Energy Investment Program   125

Notes   132

References   139

Index   145

Acknowledgments   159

About the Author   163

1 Introduction: The Global Green Energy Challenge

Here is the fundamental challenge we confront with climate change. As of 2012, total annual greenhouse gas emissions were at roughly 45 billion metric tons of mostly carbon dioxide (CO_2), along with smaller amounts of methane, nitrous oxide, and other gases. The Intergovernmental Panel on Climate Change (IPCC) estimates that to stabilize the global average temperature at its current level of around 60.3° Fahrenheit, which is 3.6° above the pre-industrial average of 56.7°, total emissions will need to fall 40 percent within twenty years, to 27 billion tons annually, and 80 percent by 2050, to about 9 billion tons.[1]

We are not on track to meet these goals. If global economic growth follows roughly the trajectory it has taken over the past century, and especially the past fifty years, global emissions will not fall at all, but rather increase persistently with time.

What happens if we fail to meet the IPCC's emission reduction targets? Nobody knows for certain. But the overwhelming consensus from leading climate scientists is clear about what we should take to be serious possibilities. Climate scientist Kerry Emanuel of MIT has offered the following perspectives in his book *What We Know About Climate Change*:

- "There will be more frequent and intense heat waves, previously fertile areas in the subtropics may become barren, and blights may seriously affect both natural vegetation and crops."
- "Comparatively small shifts in precipitation and temperature can exert considerable pressure on governments and social systems whose failure to respond could lead to famine, disease, mass emigrations, and political instability."
- "Were the entire Greenland ice cap to melt, sea level would increase by 22 feet, flooding many coastal regions, including much of Southern Florida and lower Manhattan. Eleven of the fifteen largest cities in the world are located estuaries and all would be affected."
- "The 2005 hurricane season was the most active on record, corresponding to the record warmth of the tropical Atlantic. . . . Globally, tropical cyclones cause staggering misery and loss of life (2012, pp. 55-57)."

This book proposes measures to reduce that portion of CO_2 emissions produced by burning fossil fuels—oil, coal and natural gas—to generate energy. Climate change cannot be entirely blamed on we humans consuming oil, coal, and natural gas to generate energy. But people consuming fossil fuels for energy can be blamed for about 80 percent of the problem. More precisely, of the 45 billion tons of total global greenhouse gas (GHG) emissions in 2012, about 82 percent resulted from energy production and consumption. This includes about 30 billion tons of CO_2 emissions generated by burning oil, coal, and natural gas, equaling about two-thirds of total global GHG emissions.[2] It also includes about 3 billion tons produced by generating energy from what we can call "high-emissions" bioenergy sources, including the burning of wood or ethanol derived from corn or sugarcane.[3] Producing energy also generates about 4 tons of methane and nitrous oxide emissions, as non-CO_2 sources of green gas emissions. Agricultural production is the other major source of GHG emissions, accounting for about 13 percent in total, in about equal shares of methane and nitrous oxide.[4]

Controlling methane and nitrous oxide emissions from agricultural as well as other, smaller sources of emissions will of course be necessary to advance a successful global climate stabilization project. But this book will focus on the roughly 80 percent of the problem that we can solve by burning less oil, coal and natural gas, as well as, to a lesser extent, high-emissions renewables. To achieve this goal, it is plausible to start with the premise that global CO_2 emissions will need to fall by at least the same rate as overall GHG emissions—40 percent within twenty years, and 80 percent by 2050. This means that global CO_2 emissions will need to be no more than about 20 billion tons by 2035 and 6.7 billion tons by 2050.

The emissions reduction target is the first and most important element of a transformational clean energy project. But to be successful, it is imperative that this project also commit to expanding economic well-being throughout the world. We need to start here with job opportunities. The reason is straightforward. Does someone in your family have a job, and if so, how much does it pay? For the overwhelming majority of the world's population, how one answers these two questions determines, more than anything else, what one's standard of living will be. We therefore must explore in depth how any climate stabilization program will impact job opportunities throughout the globe.

There is a widely held belief that protecting the environment and expanding job opportunities are necessarily conflicting goals, that therefore impose severe and unavoidable trade-offs in all regions of the world. This position is wrong. I advance here a unified program that can realistically achieve the IPCC's emission reduction targets while at the same time generating widespread and broadly shared economic benefits. In particular, this program will expand employment opportunities in all regions of the globe, relative to an economic trajectory that maintains our current dependence on a fossil-fuel dominated energy infrastructure.

It is especially critical that developing countries be able to raise living standards for working people and the poor as the global clean energy transformation proceeds. Reducing opportunities for higher living standards in the name of climate stabilization is simply not viable. Most importantly, there is no reasonable standard of fairness that can justify working people and the poor sacrificing opportunities for rising living standards to achieve climate stabilization. In addition, any climate stabilization program that would entail reducing mass living standards will face formidable political resistance. This, in turn, will create unacceptable delays in advancing an effective climate stabilization program. My aim is to show how the clean energy transformation, employment expansion, and poverty reduction can advance in mutually supportive ways, throughout the world.

The basics of my proposal are simple. The global economy can achieve the IPCC's twenty-year emissions reduction target if most countries—especially those with either large GDPs or populations—devote between 1.5 and 2 percent per year of GDP to investments in energy efficiency and clean, low-emissions renewable energy sources. The consumption of oil, coal and natural gas will also need to fall by about 35 percent over this same twenty-year period—i.e. at an average 2.2 percent rate of decline per year. In its essentials, just to emphasize again, that is the *entire* global clean energy program I am proposing.

Of course, many critical issues need to be worked through within this broad framework. To begin with, energy efficiency investments in all regions of the world will need to span each country's stock of buildings, transportation systems, and industrial processes. Efficiency levels will need to rise, among other places, in office towers and homes, with residential lighting and cooking equipment, and in the performance of automobiles and provision of public transportation. Expanding the supply of clean renewable energy will require major investments in solar, wind, geothermal, and small-scale hydro power, as well as in low-emissions bioenergy sources, such as ethanol from switchgrass, agricultural wastes, and waste grease. Expanding supply from *high*-emissions bioenergy sources such as corn-based ethanol and wood will not reduce CO_2 emissions at all.

There is no reason, in principle, that countries that invest between 1.5 and 2 percent of GDP in clean energy should experience any difficulties in maintaining healthy rates of economic growth. Here again, the reasons are straightforward. To begin with, energy efficiency investments, by definition, generate savings in energy costs. Through these savings, energy efficiency investments pay for themselves, within about three years, on average. Meanwhile, for most clean renewable energy sources, the average costs of providing energy are now at rough parity with fossil fuels. This means that energy consumers who substitute clean renewables for fossil fuel energy sources will not need to pay more to heat and cool their homes and offices, travel by cars, buses or trains, or operate industrial machinery.

Not all clean renewable energy sources are at cost parity with fossil fuels. Solar energy is the most significant case in point. But solar energy costs are falling sharply as increased investment levels spur innovation. The International Renewable Energy Agency (IRENA) estimates that average costs of solar-generated electricity should fall by about 40 percent between 2012 and 2020 and will continue to fall as solar production expands globally.

These new investments in energy efficiency and clean renewable energy will also generate a significant expansion of job opportunities throughout all regions of the globe. As noted above, this fact contradicts the widely-held view that climate stabilization policies must mean job losses for working people. Yet the reality that clean energy investments generate more job opportunities relative to maintaining existing fossil-fuel infrastructures has nothing to do with the environmental benefits of clean energy investments per se. It is rather due to the fact that, in all regions of the world, clean energy investment projects consistently generate more jobs for a given amount of spending than maintaining or expanding a country's existing fossil fuel energy infrastructure. Research that I have conducted with co-authors has found that this relationship holds in a wide range of countries, at all levels of development, including Brazil, China, Germany, India, Indonesia, South Africa, South Korea, Spain and the United States.

Pushing CO_2 emissions down will also generate major environmental and public health benefits beyond those achieved through climate stabilization itself. For example, a survey of thirty-seven studies from around the world found that the health benefits of reducing CO_2 emissions would average about $49 for every ton of emissions reduced. By some directly quantifiable economic measures, this benefit level is roughly on par with the climate stabilization benefits themselves.[5] While this book focuses on climate stabilization and job creation, it is important to also keep in mind these further environmental and health benefits.

Scaling the Clean Energy Investment Project

How much will we need to expand clean energy investment to bring the total within 1.5–2 percent of global GDP? As of 2013, global GDP was $87 trillion (at purchasing power parity). Thus, the range of 1.5–2 percent of global GDP is between $1.3 and $1.7 trillion at current GDP levels. As a midpoint figure of $1.5 trillion, this would mean that throughout the global economy, investments would be at about $750 billion each for clean renewables and energy efficiency investments, assuming new investment funds were divided evenly between these two sectors. If spending were instead divided at something closer to 1 percent for renewables and 0.5 percent for energy efficiency, as will probably be appropriate in most country settings, that will entail devoting about $1 trillion for renewables and $500 billion for energy efficiency at the current global GDP level. These clean energy investment figures would also increase annually, corresponding with the growth of global GDP.

According to the most recent credible data, total global renewable investments were at $227 billion in 2011 and energy efficiency investments were between $150 and $300 billion.[6] This totals $377–$527 billion, or 0.4–0.6 percent of global GDP. In other words, current global investments in clean energy are already at roughly 30 percent of where they need to be to reach $1.5 trillion. It is clear that a great deal needs to be accomplished to raise global clean energy investments up to 1.5–2 percent of global GDP. But with current global investments already at 0.4–0.6 percent of global GDP, getting up even to the higher-end range of 2 percent of GDP is not so far out of reach as to appear infeasible.

Increasing global clean energy investments by about 1.5 percent of global GDP relative to current levels will require the development of effective industrial policies for countries at all levels of development. This will entail large-scale public investments in clean energy—for example, to raise efficiency standards in government-owned buildings, and to substitute renewables for oil, coal and natural gas within the government's own energy purchases. Abundant and affordable financing for private businesses will also be critical. The situation with energy efficiency investments makes this clear. Even if efficiency investments pay for themselves within three years, they still require financiers to put up the funds to cover up-front costs. Moreover, loans for energy efficiency investments need to be structured to enable borrowers to easily pay back their loans on the basis of their annual energy savings.

In conjunction with the need for a major expansion in energy efficiency and clean renewable energy investments worldwide, it is also the case that the burning of oil, coal and natural gas will need to contract dramatically. As noted above, in order to meet the IPCC emissions reduction target over the next twenty years, total fossil fuel consumption will need to fall, as of 2035, by around 35 percent relative to its 2012 level—i.e. at a rate of decline of about 2.2 percent per year. The extent of these cuts is especially formidable, given that they will occur while the global economy is still growing every year. Within the context of a growing global economy, standard forecasts estimate that fossil fuel consumption would not fall *at all* over the next twenty years, but rather increase in the range of 50 percent relative to current levels.

Of course, fossil fuel companies won't accept a 35 percent cut in their market sales without a bitter fight. According to a recent study by Carbon Tracker and the Grantham Institute at the London School of Economics, the privately-owned fossil fuel assets that are now in the ground will lose about $3 trillion in value due to retrenchments that are necessary to advance a viable climate stabilization project.[7] But as we will see in the coming chapters, there is no alternative to these retrenchments if we are going to make a serious commitment to stabilizing the climate. This conclusion is unaffected by whether new fossil fuel reserves are discovered, such as the so-called "pre-salt" deposits in Brazil or elsewhere. It is also unaffected by whether new technologies, such as hydraulic fracturing—i.e. "fracking"—are employed to produce fossil fuel energy more cheaply.

Workers tied to the oil, coal, and natural gas industries will inevitably face major job losses as a consequence, even while these losses will be spread out over time. The communities in which these workers and their families live will experience unavoidable hardships. Political movements committed to climate stabilization therefore need to force governments in all countries to generously support these workers, as well as their families and communities, as they transition into new jobs and industries. In most countries, the energy efficiency and clean renewable energy sectors will be among the most important new areas of expanding job opportunities.

Global CO_2 Emissions Projections for 2035

The magnitude of the challenges ahead become clear when we consider the CO_2 emission level projections for 2035 by two of the largest and most influential organizations that develop models to address this question: the United States Department of Energy's Energy Information Agency (EIA), which produces an annual *International Energy Outlook*, and the OECD's International Energy Agency (IEA), which publishes an annual *World Energy Outlook*.

Table 1.1 presents the most recent projections of the EIA and IEA for world CO_2 emissions levels under various scenarios. The table shows two of the EIA's scenarios: their "Reference" case, which is the EIA's assessment of the most likely level of global emissions in 2035, and their alternative rapid economic growth scenario, in which they assume that average annual GDP growth

Table 1.1 Projected World CO_2 Emissions Levels for 2035 by U.S. Energy Information Agency and International Energy Agency

Agency and Scenario	2035 CO_2 Emissions Projections
U.S. Energy Information Agency (EIA)	
■ Reference Case *(3.6% average GDP growth)*	43.7 billion tons
■ Rapid Economic Growth *4.0% average GDP growth)*	50.7 billion tons
International Energy Agency (IEA)	
■ Current Policies Scenario	43.4 billion tons
■ New Policies Scenario	37.2 billion tons
■ 450/Low Carbon Scenario	22.3 billion tons

Sources: EIA *International Energy Statistics* website; IEA (2014). The IEA projections for their Current Policies and 450 scenarios are midpoints between their 2030 and 2040 projections.

through 2035 rises from 3.6 percent under the Reference case to 4.0 percent. As we see in the table, under these two cases, the EIA projects that total global CO_2 emissions will range between 43.7–50.7 billion tons. These levels are between 120–150 percent higher than the IPCC twenty-year target of 20 billion tons.

The IEA provides three projections: a "Current Policies" case, which is equivalent to the EIA's Reference case, along with a "New Policies Case" and a "450/Low Carbon" case. (The "450" refers to a GHG atmospheric measurement of 450 parts per million, a level some climate scientists believe is sufficiently low to achieve climate stabilization.) The IEA describes its New Policies case as taking into account "broad policy commitments and plans that have already been implemented to address energy-related challenges as well as those that have been announced." But it also "assumes only cautious implementation of current commitments and plans." The 450/Low Carbon case, by contrast, sets out "an energy pathway that is consistent with a 50 percent chance of meeting the goal of limiting the increase in average global temperature to 2° C compared with pre-industrial levels."[8] In other words, the IEA believes that its 450/Low Carbon case provides a 50 percent chance for the world to control climate change.

As Table 1.1 shows, under the IEA's 2035 Current Policies case—as with the EIA's Reference case—global CO_2 emissions are at 43.4 billion tons. This is, again, more than twice as high as the 20 billion ton target for controlling climate change. The situation is only modestly improved in the IEA's New Policies case, which projects 2035 CO_2 emissions to total 37.2 billion tons. Even under the 450/Low Carbon case, the IEA projects 22.3 billion tons by 2035. This is a dramatic improvement relative to all the other cases, but it is still 12 percent higher than the 20 billion ton target for 2035, and it offers only a 50 percent chance of success.

Could it be more clear from these EIA and IEA projections that we are courting ecological disaster unless we advance a full-scale global clean energy program, starting now? This means a program that is substantially more ambitious than even the IEA's 450/Low Carbon scenario.

Global and Country-Level Perspectives

As I noted above, 2012 global CO_2 emissions were at roughly 33 billion tons. It is important now to consider these overall emissions figures from a range of perspectives, including those of individual countries. The data in Table 1.2 provide a starting point for this more detailed analysis.

As we see in Table 1.2, in 2012, total global energy consumption amounted to about 529 quadrillion BTUs (Q-BTUs) from

Table 1.2 Energy Consumption and CO_2 Emissions Levels for World and Selected Countries, 2012

	Energy Consumption		CO_2 Emissions	
	Total Primary Energy Consumption *(Q-BTUs)*	Per-capita energy consumption *(Millions BTUs)*	Total CO_2 Emissions *(Billions of metric tons)*	Per capita CO_2 Emissions *(Metric tons)*
World	**528.8**	**74.2**	**32.72**	**4.6**
China	110.6	77.5	8.55	6.4
United States	95.1	312.8	5.27	16.7
Brazil	12.1	60.2	0.50	2.5
Germany	13.5	165.4	0.78	9.8
India	23.9	19.7	1.83	1.5
Indonesia	11.5	25.7	0.46	1.8
South Africa	5.7	115.4	0.47	8.9
South Korea	11.5	231.9	0.66	13.1
Spain	6.0	127.1	0.31	6.6

Source: EIA website.

all energy sources—including fossil fuels, all renewable sources, and nuclear power. (Burning a wood match to its end generates about 1 BTU of energy. The box below offers examples of how much energy is provided in 1 Q-BTU.) Fossil fuels provide a total of 81 percent of all energy resources, with oil at 31, coal at 29, and natural gas at 21 percent. Over 90 percent of the 33 billion tons of CO_2 emissions derive from these three sources. The remaining 10 percent comes from burning wood, corn ethanol, and other high-emissions bioenergy sources.

How Much Energy Does One Q-BTU Provide in the United States?

Residential Energy Consumption: 1 Q-BTU equals the total average annual energy consumption for the residences of 10 million U.S. households. This corresponds roughly to the annual residential energy consumption for all households in Pennsylvania and Ohio combined.

Automobile Travel: 1 Q-BTU can provide enough energy for 61 million round-trip automobile journeys between New York City and Los Angeles.

Power Plants: 1 Q-BTU is the amount of electricity generated in one year by 408 averaged-sized U.S. power plants. This is about 7 percent of all U.S. power plants. It is approximately equal to the amount of electricity consumed in one year in Michigan, Virginia, and Colorado combined.

Coal Supply: 1 Q-BTU is roughly equal to the energy contained in 40 million tons of coal. This is the amount of coal that would be loaded onto a freight train that stretches from New York City to Fairbanks, Alaska.

Numbers of calories: 1 Q-BTU contains just over 250 trillion calories. This is roughly equal to the amount of calories contained in 1 trillion McDonald's hamburgers. If each of the world's 7.1 billion people ate 140 hamburgers—one a day for twenty weeks—this would equal the amount of calories contained in 1 Q-BTU.

Source: see Pollin et al. 2014, p. 17.

China and the United States lead the world in both energy consumption and CO_2 emissions. As Table 1.2 shows, China is consuming 110.6 Q-BTUs annually, or 21 percent of the global total, while the U.S. is consuming 95 Q-BTUs, or 18 percent of the total. Thus, together, China and the United States account for 39 percent of world energy consumption. In terms of carbon emissions, China is again highest, at 8.6 billion tons, while the United States is at 5.3 billion tons, together accounting for 42 percent of all global carbon emissions. Obviously, any serious global climate stabilization project must begin with these two countries.

But Table 1.2 also makes clear that the challenges of advancing an effective and fair global climate stabilization project will have distinct features with respect to these two countries. The United States is an advanced industrial economy with a per capita energy consumption rate among the highest in the world for large population countries, at 313 million BTUs per capita.[9] China, by contrast, despite its historically unprecedented growth over the past thirty-five years, is still a developing country by many measures. China's per capita energy consumption, at 77.5 million BTUs, is roughly a fourth of that of the U.S. and on par with the global average of 74.1 million BTUs. Similarly, per capita CO_2 emissions in China are at 6.5 tons, while the figure for the U.S. is nearly three times higher, at 16.7 tons.

The cases of the United States and China also underscore another fundamental fact. As important as these countries are for achieving global climate stabilization, they still contribute, in combination, well less than half of overall global CO_2 emissions. As a result, we must be equally concerned to develop policies that apply to all other countries throughout the globe, including, significantly, the other countries listed in Table 1.2: Brazil, Germany, India, Indonesia, Spain South Africa, and

South Korea. Moreover, as with the comparative situations for the United States and China, the differences among these seven other countries are dramatic. For example, per capita energy consumption in Germany is 165.4 million BTUs, 45 percent below the U.S. level but nearly nine times India's and seven times Indonesia's. Per capita emissions in Germany, at 9.8 tons, are 42 percent lower than the U.S. figure of 16.7 tons, but are more than six times those for India and Indonesia.

Specifying the Climate Stabilization Challenge

Table 1.2 shows that average global CO_2 emissions in 2012 are at 4.6 tons per capita, ranging between 1.5 tons for India to 16.7 tons for the United States. These figures provide a critical metric for clarifying the scale and types of policy initiatives that will be necessary for stabilizing the global climate.

In particular, we can express our twenty-year goal of bringing global emissions down to 20 billion tons in terms of this measure. With global population expected to rise to about 8.7 billion by 2035, carbon emissions will need to be at no more than 2.3 tons per capita by 2035. The question is how to achieve this reduction in a way that is also supportive of rising living standards and declining poverty rates.

This challenge becomes especially sharp when we consider the current pattern in the relationship between per capita GDP levels and emissions. On average, per capita emissions rise substantially as countries become richer. We can see this pattern clearly in Table 1.3 (p. 16), which divides all countries with populations exceeding 5 million into four broad income categories, as defined by the World Bank.[10] Low-income countries, with a total population of 709 million people, operate with average

Table 1.3 World Per Capita GDP Groupings and CO_2 Emissions Levels, 2012

Per Capita GDP Categories	Average GDP per Capita (2012 U.S. Dollars)	Total Population	Average Emissions per Capita (Metric tons)
Low Income (GDP below $1,045)	$632	709 million	0.2 tons
Lower-Middle Income (GDP between $1,045 - $4,125)	$2,355	2.5 billion	1.3 tons
Upper-Middle Income (GDP between $4,125 - $12,746)	$7,640	2.3 billion	4.8 tons
High-Income (GDP above $12,746)	$38,133	1.3 billion	9.5 tons

Source: World Bank (2015), Tables 1.1, 3.8, 3.9, and authors' calculations of under-lying metadata. Countries with populations less than 4 million omitted from sample.

emissions level of 0.2 tons per capita. The figure then rises to 1.3 tons for lower-middle income countries, 4.8 tons for upper-middle income countries, and 9.5 tons for high-income countries. On average, then, the 1.3 billion residents of high-income countries generate 7.3 times more emissions than the 2.5 billion people living in lower-middle income countries, and 48 times more emissions than the 709 million people living in low-income countries.

There is some significant variation within these average figures. For example, among high-income countries, France, Switzerland, and Sweden operate with emissions levels at roughly 5.5 tons per capita, about half the average for high-income countries. Among upper-middle income countries, Brazil stands out for already operating at 2.3 average tons per capita—i.e. at the level the overall global economy needs to reach by 2035. There are also some especially poor performers that we need to recognize. Canada, Australia, and the United States stand out among high-income countries with per capita emissions levels that are between 7 and 8 times higher than the 2.3 average we need to reach by 2035.

Nevertheless, the overall perspective coming out of these figures is clear. First, if there is to be any chance of the global economy achieving the average emissions target of 2.3 tons per capita by 2035, average emissions in the high-income countries will need to fall dramatically over the next twenty years from their current level of just under 10 tons per capita. Emissions will also need to fall sharply among the upper-middle income countries from their current level of 4.8 tons per capita.

Of course, the situation is completely different for the low- and lower-middle income countries, which includes 46 percent of the world's population and in which average emissions are at 0.2 and 1.3 tons respectively. It is imperative that living standards for working people and the poor in these countries improve substantially over the next twenty years. But how much will emissions levels have to rise in these countries as a result of improving living standards? More specifically, how much can emissions levels rise in these countries before it becomes unrealistic for the global economy overall to achieve the 2035 target of 2.3 tons per capita, even if the rich and upper-middle income countries succeed in making sharp emissions cuts?

Answering these questions inevitably pushes us into the realm of what is both fair and realistic as a global climate stabilization program. There is no escaping the conclusion that, to date, fossil fuel energy consumption by people in high-income countries is the single most important cause of climate change. Any fair climate stabilization program must require more of these countries. The U.S. stands out here, given that it is, by far, the largest economy in which per capita emissions are more than 3 times the global average.

Should we therefore conclude that the U.S. must, within twenty years, drive down its own emissions to 2.3 tons per capita, the global target for 2035? That would mean a cut in U.S. emissions by 86 percent relative to its present level of 16.7 tons per capita. There is a solid ethical case for this. But there is absolutely no chance that it could actually happen. The central ethical question should therefore be: what can the U.S. realistically accomplish that can also contribute the most in advancing global climate stabilization over the next twenty years? This is a question on which I hope the discussions over the next chapters of this book will shed some light. We will return to this question of fairness in the concluding Chapter 8, with the materials we cover in the previous chapters serving as our necessary background.

Options for Reducing Global CO_2 Emissions

Despite wide differences in levels of development across the globe, there are still only a limited number of ways in which any country can control its CO_2 emissions while maintaining energy consumption sufficient to support rising living standards. These are:

1. Reduce absolute energy consumption, either through conservation or efficiency improvements.
2. Among fossil fuel energy sources, increase the proportion of natural gas consumption relative to coal, since carbon emissions from burning natural gas are about half those from coal.

3. Invest in the development and commercialization of some combination of the following technologies:
    - Clean renewables, including solar, wind, hydro, geo-thermal and some types of bioenergy
    - Nuclear power
    - Carbon Capture and Sequestration (CCS) processes in generating coal, oil, and natural gas-powered energy

I examine each of these options in Chapters 2 through 4. My conclusion out of these chapters is that, for a wide range of reasons, only two of these options are capable of playing a major role in advancing a successful global climate stabilization project. These are: investments to raise energy efficiency levels, and investments to expand capacity in clean renewable energy sources. This is why pursuing these two options will constitute the core of the 1.5–2 percent of global GDP clean energy investment project. It will also be the basis on which we are able to show, in Chapter 5, how global emissions can realistically be cut to 20 billion tons—i.e. 2.3 tons per capita—within twenty years. Understanding the nature of this clean energy investment project will then, in turn, enable us in Chapter 6 to evaluate the employment effects of these investments relative to maintaining the existing global energy infrastructure dominated by oil, coal, and natural gas. Chapter 7 then explores policy approaches that are capable of delivering a successful global clean energy project over the next twenty years. I also discuss an approach which I do not believe is viable, even though it has attracted considerable support among environmentalists. This is to deliberately forego economic growth or even force an overall contraction in the level of economic activity—i.e. undertake, as the term has emerged, economic "de-growth." As we will see, the de-growth approach is incapable of playing a major role in reducing global CO_2 emissions, while it would generate major losses in economic well-being for working people and the poor throughout the world.

In the concluding Chapter 8, I begin by posing the question: What if mainstream climate scientists are wrong? Would we then be wasting enormous sums of money by mounting a global clean energy investment project? The short answer is "no." This is because the clean energy investment project needs to be understood as a kind of global climate change insurance policy. These investments will be protecting us against contingencies, not against outcomes that we can predict with 100 percent certainty. I will then close Chapter 8 by returning to the fundamental questions of fairness that are at stake within any global climate stabilization program. This includes the question of how to deal with owners of fossil fuel companies who will face major losses in profitability to the extent that the global clean energy project succeeds.

2 Prospects for Fossil Fuels and Nuclear Power

The most basic cause of global climate change is fossil fuel consumption. We burn fossil fuels to heat, light, and cool buildings, to cook food, to commute to jobs, to travel, and to incorporate all varieties of machinery into the operations of our workplaces and homes. As of 2012, oil, coal and natural gas consumption accounted for about 80 percent of total global energy supply and 90 percent of all CO_2 emissions. Nuclear energy, the other non-renewable energy source, provides another 5 percent of total global energy supply. Relative to fossil fuels, nuclear power provides the major benefit of generating zero emissions.

What level of fossil fuel consumption can be sustained if we are going to succeed over the next twenty years in bringing fossil-fuel generated CO_2 emissions down from the current level of 33 billion tons to 20 billion tons? To answer this question, we first need to establish how much CO_2 is generated when we burn oil, coal, and natural gas to produce a given amount of energy—for example, one Q-BTU. Based on these figures, we can consider how to use non-renewable energy sources to deliver significant cuts in CO_2 emissions. As we will see, the options here include fuel switching (from coal to natural gas), advancing carbon capture and sequestration (CCS) technologies as components of fossil fuel production systems, and expanding nuclear energy as the emissions-free source of non-renewable energy.

The data in Table 2.1 provide a good framework for considering the issues at hand. As the first column shows, oil is the most heavily consumed fossil fuel, at 38 percent of the total 433 Q-BTUs of fossil fuel energy supply. Coal accounts for 36 percent of total supply, while natural gas is at 26 percent.

These three energy sources vary substantially in the CO_2 emissions they generate per Q-BTU of energy. As we see in the second column, coal is the dirtiest energy source, generating about 93 million tons of CO_2 per Q-BTU of energy. Oil is 35 percent cleaner than coal, at 69 million tons of CO_2 per Q-BTU of energy. Natural gas is somewhat cleaner still; at 59 million tons of CO_2 per Q-BTU of energy, it is 57 percent cleaner than coal and 17 percent cleaner than oil.

Table 2.1 World Energy Consumption and CO_2 Emissions from Fossil Fuels, 2012

	Total Consumption Q-BTUs	Emissions per Q-BTU *millions of metric tons*	Total CO_2 Emissions *billions of metric tons* *(= column 1*2) * (1,000)*
Oil	166 *(38% of total)*	69.3	11.5 *(35% of total)*
Coal	154 *(36% of total)*	93.1	14.4 *(44% of total)*
Natural Gas	113 *(26% of total)*	59.2	6.7 *(21% of total)*
TOTALS	433	75.1	32.7

Source: IEA (2014) pp. 606, 608. Emissions figures adjusted upward by 3 percent to harmonize with World Bank and EIA emissions data. See Chapter 1, endnote 4 for details.

Fuel Switching and Fracking

The general argument for switching from coal to natural gas is evident from the data in Table 2.1. Natural gas could be used as a substitute for coal for generating electricity, which is the primary use of both energy sources. For every Q-BTU of electricity generated by natural gas rather than coal, CO_2 emissions would fall by nearly 34 million tons.

The case for coal-to-natural gas switching has been bolstered in recent years by the expanding use of hydraulic fracturing technology—"fracking"—that extracts natural gas from shale rock. Through fracking technology, natural gas can be mined more cheaply than coal, which in turn lowers the costs of producing natural-gas-fired electricity. For example, the U.S. Energy Information Agency projects that in 2017 the total cost of natural gas–fired electricity will be 6.6 cents per kilowatt hour versus 9.8 cents for coal-fired electricity.

But pursuing a large-scale coal-to-natural gas switching faces two fundamental problems. The first is that most credible research finds that fracking consistently produces serious environmental costs. In particular, fracking has been demonstrated to contaminate drinking water with methane gas in aquifers overlying shale formations. Duke University ecologist Robert Jackson and his co-authors examined fracking sites in Pennsylvania and New York. They found that

> Based on groundwater analyses of 60 private water wells in the region, methane concentrations were found to be 17 times higher on average in areas with active drilling and extraction than in non-active areas, with some drinking-water wells having

concentrations of methane well above the "immediate action" hazard level.[1]

As a result of such negative findings, New York and Vermont
have banned fracking, and other U.S. states and municipalities
have either imposed temporary moratoria or are seriously considering such measures. In Europe, countries that have banned fracking include France and Bulgaria, which have the largest deposits
of exploitable shale rock resources on the continent. Germany
now operates with what amounts to an effective ban. The Czech
Republic, Northern Ireland, and the regions of Cantabria in Spain
and Fribourg in Switzerland have also established bans, while
Romania and Luxembourg have declared moratoria.

Fracking also increases the likelihood of methane leaking into
the environment during the process of producing natural gas,
before the gas is burned to generate energy. Recent research has
concluded that when more than 5.4 percent of the gas produced
leaks into the atmosphere, the impact eliminates any environmental benefit from burning natural gas relative to coal for electricity generation. One such study found that, on average, leakage
rates from natural gas production are already in the range of 5.4
percent. Another study focusing on fracking operations in Texas
and North Dakota found leakage rates in the range of 9 to 10 percent. If such rates were sustained, the overall emissions impact
for natural gas—including methane leakages as well as CO_2 production from combustion—would be worse than that for burning
coal.[2]

But even if water contamination risks were negligible and
methane leakage could be cut to insignificant levels, the emissions benefits from coal-to-natural gas switching would be modest at best. We can see this clearly by considering again the data
in Table 2.1. Assume, for illustration, a completely unrealistic

scenario in which 100 percent of coal consumption in 2012—all 154 Q-BTUs—is replaced by natural gas. The 13.9 billion tons of coal-generated CO_2 emissions would be replaced by 8.9 tons from natural gas (i.e. 154 Q-BTUs times 57.5 million tons per Q-BTU with natural gas). This would bring overall emissions for 2012 down by 16 percent—less than half the reduction needed to achieve the IPCC target by 2035. A 50 percent coal-to-natural gas fuel switch, still implausibly large, would end up reducing CO_2 emissions by only 8 percent.

What these exercises demonstrate is that there are likely to be very little, if any, benefits attainable through relying on coal-to-natural gas fuel switching as a primary strategy for reducing CO_2 emissions dramatically within the next twenty years.

Carbon Capture and Sequestration

Carbon capture and sequestration (CCS) encompasses a number of specific technologies that capture CO_2 from point sources, such as power plants and other industrial facilities. The captured CO_2 is then transported, usually through pipelines, and stored indefinitely in subsurface geological formations.

The case for CCS is straightforward: the development of effective CCS technologies would allow the continued use of fossil fuel energy without releasing such high levels of CO_2. At the same time, as surveyed forcefully by Joseph Romm, arguably the most prominent climate change analyst in the United States, there are four major problems associated with CCS technologies, which together render the approach unsuitable as a major clean-energy strategy, either for the short- or long-term.[3] As described by Romm, the four problems are:

- *Cost.* Coal plants with CCS are very expensive. For example, a 2012 study by the U.S. Congressional Budget Office found that plants equipped with CCS technology have capital costs averaging 76 percent higher than non-CCS plants.
- *Timing.* The world does not even have a single large-scale coal plant with CCS in operation. Rather, most governments and most U.S. utilities have scaled back, delayed, or cancelled their planned CCS projects.
- *Scale.* For CCS to play a major role in climate stabilization would require a flow of CO_2 into the ground equal to the current flow of oil out of the ground. That would require, by itself, re-creating the equivalent of the planet's entire oil delivery infrastructure.
- *Permanence and transparency.* It would be necessary to create an international regime for certifying, monitoring, verifying, and inspecting geologic repositories of carbon, equivalent to the U.N. weapons inspections systems. At present, there is no place in the world with knowledge as to how to monitor and verify underground CO_2 storage. Romm suggests that it could take a decade just to set up such a system. By way of comparison, the United States has not been able to certify a single storage facility for high-level radioactive waste after two decades of trying.

In addition to the issues highlighted by Romm, there are also broader environmental concerns. Leakage from underground CO_2 repositories could contaminate ground water, and thereby, drinking water. Leakages could also entail new releases of the very CO_2 emissions the technology is designed to mitigate. Still another issue is the environmental damage from continued coal extraction through mountaintop removal and strip mining.

Considering all these factors, the IEA's 2013 *World Energy Outlook* presents a highly pessimistic assessment of the prospects for CCS:

> Progress in developing CCS has been disappointingly slow. There is, to date, no commercial CCS application in the power sector or in energy-intensive industries. Beyond technological and economic challenges, there could be legal challenges related to the potential for CO_2 gas escape from underground storage.[4]

It is possible that major technological breakthroughs will create a much more favorable outlook for CCS than those presented in summary assessments by Romm and the IEA. But the evidence for any such major breakthroughs does not presently exist.

Nuclear Power

As of 2012, nuclear power provided 25 Q-BTUs of energy throughout the global economy, which represented about 4.8 percent of global energy supply. Eighty-five percent of global nuclear power supply is generated within the OECD economies.

Nuclear power provides the obvious important benefit that it does not directly generate GHG emissions or air pollution of any kind. At the same time, mining and refining uranium ore and making reactor fuel require large amounts of energy, and nuclear power plants utilize large amounts of metal and concrete as construction materials, which require large amounts of energy to manufacture. As a result, nuclear power does generate some secondary fossil fuels emissions.

It is difficult to reach firm conclusions about the extensiveness of such secondary emissions effects. However, even if we assume a best-case scenario that such effects are negligible, in terms of full cycle emission from generating nuclear energy, we still need to recognize the other longstanding environmental and public safety issues associated with nuclear energy. These include:

- *Radioactive wastes.* These wastes include uranium mill tailings, spent reactor fuel, and other wastes, which, according to the EIA, "can remain radioactive and dangerous to human health for thousands of years."[5]
- *Storage of spent reactor fuel and power plant decommissioning.* Spent reactor fuel assemblies are highly radioactive and must be stored in specially designed pools or storage containers. When a nuclear power plant stops operating, the decommissioning process involves safely removing the plant from service and reducing radioactivity to a level that permits other uses of the property.
- *Nuclear reactor meltdowns.* An uncontrolled nuclear reaction at a nuclear plant can result in widespread contamination of air and water with radioactivity for hundreds of miles around a reactor.
- *Nuclear proliferation.* Nuclear energy can obviously be used to produce deadly weapons as well as electricity. The proliferation of nuclear energy production creates dangers that this capacity could be acquired by organizations—governments or otherwise—who would use that energy as instruments of war or terror.

The critical question here is: Can a global nonproliferation regime be established such that a significantly expanded reliance on nuclear energy for electricity will not diminish safety and security? A recent extensive survey by authorities from a wide range of perspectives concludes that "the technical, economic and political factors that will determine whether future generations will have more nuclear power without more nuclear proliferation are both exceedingly complex and interrelated."[6] In short, there is simply no way to ensure that a significantly increasing use worldwide of nuclear energy for electricity can be achieved without also increasing the dangers associated with nuclear power as a weapon.

Even while recognizing these problems with nuclear energy, it is still the case, as noted above, that nuclear power supplies roughly five percent of global energy supply. For decades, these risks were considered relatively small and manageable when balanced against its benefits. However, this view was upended in the aftermath of the March 2011 nuclear meltdown at the Fukushima Daiichi power plant in Japan, which resulted from the massive 9.0 Tohuku earthquake and tsunami.

The full effects of the Fukushima meltdown cannot possibly be known for some time. As of August 2013, two and a half years after the meltdown, the situation deteriorated seriously. Japan's Nuclear Regulatory Authority stated, as reported by Reuters, "that it feared more storage tanks were leaking contaminated water...Water in the latest leak is so contaminated that a person standing close to it for an hour would receive five times the annual recommended limit for nuclear workers."[7]

In its 2013 *International Energy Outlook*, the EIA acknowledges that Fukushima has intensified concerns worldwide about the viability of expanding, or even maintaining, nuclear energy as a major power source:

> The Fukushima Daiichi disaster could have long-term implications for the future of world nuclear power development in general. Even China . . . halted approval processes for all new reactors until the country's nuclear regulator completed its safety review. Germany and Switzerland announced plans to phase out or shut down their operating reactors by 2022 and 2034, respectively. . . . The uncertainty associated with nuclear power projections for Japan and for the rest of the world has increased. [8]

These safety considerations must be accorded significant weight. As such, nuclear energy cannot be seen as serving as a reliable long-term source of non-carbon emitting energy supplies. To the extent possible, it is far preferable to rely on clean renewable energy sources and advances in energy efficiency, which have much more favorable prospects compared with those for coal-to-natural gas fuel switching, carbon capture and sequestration technology, or nuclear power.

3   Prospects for Energy Efficiency

Large-scale investment in energy efficiency is the single best option available for building a global clean energy economy and achieving the IPCC's emissions reduction target over the next twenty years. The technologies required to dramatically improve energy efficiency standards are readily available. Making energy efficiency investments will also save money over time for all varieties of energy consumers in all regions of the world. Given such favorable prospects, it is natural to wonder why we aren't already making these investments. Answers to this question should become clear as we proceed.

Energy Efficiency vs. Energy Conservation

To begin with, it is important to clarify the distinction between *energy conservation* and *energy efficiency*. Energy conservation entails reducing activities that require the consumption of energy. Examples of energy conservation include traveling fewer miles, either by car, trains, buses, airplanes or water transport, and using less energy to light, heat, or cool buildings or to power equipment either in businesses or residences.

By contrast, energy efficiency entails using less energy to achieve the same, or even higher, levels of energy services from the adoption of improved technologies and practices. Examples include insulating buildings much more effectively to stabilize inside temperatures; replacing traditional incandescent light bulbs with high-efficiency LED bulbs; driving more fuel-efficient cars, or, better yet, relying increasingly on well-functioning public transportation systems for ground transportation; and reducing the amount of energy that is wasted both through generating and transmitting electricity and through operating industrial machinery.

Energy conservation does have a role to play in reducing global CO_2 emissions and stabilizing the climate. In particular, large-scale businesses, public institutions, and upper-income households in advanced economies could, for the most part, readily reduce their energy-consuming activities without significantly affecting their mode of operations or living standards. For starters, affluent consumers could drive less, travel less by airplane, and stop running their air conditioners so intensively. But for the vast majority of the world's population, one of the central drivers of rising living standards will be to significantly enhance access to low-cost energy-based services, such as well-functioning modern buildings, convenient modes of transportation, and workplaces in which the use of energy-driven machinery raises productivity. This is why energy efficiency has to play a much more important role than energy conservation in the unified global project of stabilizing the climate and raising mass living standards.

What Are the Opportunities with Energy Efficiency?

The central importance of energy efficiency is widely understood. World Bank researchers Ashok Sarkar and Jas Singh offer this overview of the central importance of energy efficiency:

> Energy efficiency is rapidly becoming a critical policy tool around the world to help meet this substantial growth in energy demand. Evidence from the past 3-4 decades of experience around the world indicate that EE programs generally entail positive and multiple benefits for the government, energy consumers, and the environment. Such programs can: conserve natural resources; reduce the environmental pollution and carbon footprint of the energy sector; reduce a country's dependence on fossil fuels, thus enhancing its energy security; ease infrastructure bottlenecks and impacts of temporary power shortfalls; and improve industrial and commercial competiveness through reducing operating costs. In terms of project economics, EE options are seen as "no regrets" policies, since their net financial cost can be negative, i.e. the measures are justified purely based on high financial returns. . . . Amongst the menu of feasible technical options currently available to help reduce the rate of growth of greenhouse gas emissions produced by the energy sector, EE technologies stand apart as the most cost-effective ones.[1]

Work by the leading business consulting firm McKinsey and Company reinforces the findings of the World Bank researchers. In a series of recent reports, McKinsey finds that there are large numbers of specific investment activities that can reduce greenhouse gases while, at the same time, generating net savings for investors. The examples they highlight include investments in lighting, consumer appliances and electronics, heating and air-conditioning systems, building insulation, electrical motors, hybrid automobiles, and waste recycling.

The McKinsey researchers further argue that while the benefits of efficiency investments can be reaped in all regions of the world and all countries, the largest benefits per dollar of expenditure are available in developing countries. As of 2010, McKinsey estimated that, using existing technologies only, developing countries could realistically slow the growth of energy demand through 2020 by more than half—from 3.4 to 1.4 percent per year—without having to reduce GDP growth at the same time. McKinsey estimates that gains in energy efficiency throughout the developing world would generate about $600 billion per year in savings on energy costs by 2020.[2] This is equal to about 10 percent of total GDP for all low- and lower-middle income countries as of 2012.

For advanced economies, the overall prospect is that large-scale efficiency investments can produce significant reductions in the *absolute* levels of their energy consumption, even while their economies grow at healthy rates. This conclusion is expressed strongly, for example, in the major 2010 study by the U.S. National Academy of Sciences (NAS), *Real Prospects for Energy Efficiency in the United States*:

> Energy efficient technologies for residences and commercial buildings, transportation and industry exist today, or are expected to be developed in the normal course of business, that could potentially save 30 percent of the energy used in the U.S.

economy while also saving money. The full deployment of cost-effective energy-efficient technologies in buildings alone could eliminate the need to add to U.S. electricity generation capacity.[3]

Of course, individual countries vary widely in their existing levels of efficiency. We can see this by reviewing some basic data on energy intensity ratios, for the world as a whole and for some selected major economies. The *energy intensity ratio* measures the energy consumed to generate a given amount of a country's total GDP. Thus, as we see in Table 3.1, the world average for the energy intensity ratio is 7.1. This means that, as a global average, 7.1 Q-BTUs are needed to produce $1 trillion of global GDP.

Among our selected major economies, Germany stands out as the most energy efficient, with a low intensity ratio of 4.1—that is, Germany consumes 4.1 Q-BTUs of energy

Table 3.1 Energy Intensity Ratios: Global Averages and Selected Countries-
Energy Intensity = Q-BTUs of energy consumed/GDP (in trillions of U.S. dollars)

WORLD AVERAGE	7.1
Germany	4.1
Spain	4.6
Brazil	5.1
USA	6.2
Indonesia	6.8
South Korea	9.8
China	12.2
India	13.3
South Africa	14.6

Sources: EIA website.

for every trillion dollars of GDP it produces. Spain and Brazil also operates at a low energy intensity ratios of 4.6 and 5.1 respectively. The most inefficient economies in our sample are China, at a 12.2 intensity ratio; India, at 13.3; and South Africa, at 14.6. South Korea also operates at a relatively high energy intensity level of 9.8, 30 percent higher than Indonesia's. It is clear that, among this group of economies, China, India, South Africa, and South Korea are primed to achieve dramatic efficiency gains through effective large-scale investments.

But it is equally critical to emphasize that even Germany— a star performer among advanced economies—recognizes that still greater efficiency advances can be achieved at reasonable costs. Thus, the German federal government's official 2010 *Energy Concept* document sets as its goal a 20 percent absolute decline in energy consumption by 2020 and a 50 percent absolute reduction by 2050. Based on this, pattern, Germany's energy intensity ratio would fall to about 2.0 by 2035.[4]

The *Concept* document places special emphasis on opportunities for energy savings in the economy's stock of buildings. As with most advanced economies, the operation of buildings is responsible for about 40 percent of all energy consumption. The *Concept* document establishes virtually zero net emissions by 2050 as Germany's goal for its entire building stock. Achieving this goal will entail significant up-front investments in energy-efficiency technologies for buildings, including the thermal shell, as well as for heating, cooling, and lighting systems. But in the end, these investments will more than pay for themselves within a reasonable time frame, given the energy savings achieved through the up-front investments.

Estimating Costs of Efficiency Gains

Estimates of the investment costs required to achieve efficiency gains vary widely. Table 3.2 summarizes findings from three sets of studies. A 2008 World Bank study puts the average costs at $1.9 billion per Q-BTU of energy savings, based on a sample of 455 projects in both industrial and developing economies. The 2010 McKinsey report estimates costs for a wide range of low- and middle-income economies to be $11 billion per Q-BTU of energy savings. And lastly, focusing just on the U.S. economy, the 2010 U.S. National Academy of Sciences volume estimated average costs for energy efficiency savings in the buildings and industrial sectors at about $29 billion per Q-BTU.

It is not surprising that average costs would be significantly higher in more advanced economies. A high proportion of efficiency investment goes to labor costs, especially

Table 3.2 Estimates of Investment Costs for Energy Efficiency Savings

Source	Regions/Countries/ Sectors Estimated	Investment Costs per Q-BTU of Savings
World Bank	455 projects in 11 industrial and developing countries	$1.9 billion per Q-BTU
McKinsey and Co.	Africa, India, Middle East, South East Asia, Eastern Europe, China	$11 billion per Q-BTU
United States National Academy of Sciences	United States	~ $29 billion per Q-BTU for buildings, industry

Sources: See Pollin et al. (2015), p. 88.

for projects that retrofit buildings and industrial equipment. However, these wide differences in cost estimates do not result simply from variations in labor and other input costs across regions and levels of development. After all, the World Bank estimate includes both industrialized and developing countries. Similarly, the McKinsey estimate—nearly six times the World Bank figure—is primarily based on developing country projects.

These alternative studies do not provide sufficiently detailed methodological discussions to enable us to identify the main factors responsible for the large differences in their estimates. But it is at least reasonable to conclude that there are likely to be substantial variations in costs when we get down to the project-by-project level. That is, the costs for energy efficiency investments that will apply in any given situation will necessarily be specific to that situation, and must be always be analyzed on a case-by-case basis.

Still, to generate some useful global perspectives on the costs of mounting a clean energy transition—the focus of Chapter 5—we will need to proceed with some general rules-of-thumb for estimating the level of savings attainable to a typical set of efficiency projects. For our purposes, it is not critical that we establish the most accurate cost estimates for achieving efficiency savings within any given country or regional setting. Rather, our aim is to evaluate the benefits from large-scale efficiency investments when we assume that, if anything, the costs are on the higher end of the range. As such, Chapter 5 will apply to the entire global economy the high-end figure from the U.S. National Academy of Sciences. In short, I will assume that to achieve 1 Q-BTU of energy efficiency savings anywhere in the world will require, on average, $30 billion in up-front investment costs.

Why Aren't Energy Consumers Picking Up Free Money?

Considering these energy efficiency cost figures, we should emphasize again that, in all cases, the payback period for such investments is generally estimated to be relatively short—in most cases, less than three years for full payback. Given this fact, the question that is often posed in evaluating the viability of energy efficiency investments is the one I raised at the outset of this chapter: if such large opportunities for cost savings exist—independent of environmental benefits—then why aren't households, businesses, and governments pouncing on them?

The first answer is that, to a considerable extent, efficiency investments *have* been embraced over the past few decades. In fact, for the world as a whole, energy efficiency improved by 31 percent between 1990 and 2011, which amounts to an average annual rate of global efficiency gains of 1.3 percent. Among individual countries, China has achieved the largest efficiency gains, improving by 164 percent between 1990 and 2011, or 4.7 percent per year. Germany's efficiency gain between 1990 and 2011 has been by 54 percent, or 2.1 percent per year.

Despite these steady efficiency gains worldwide, large-scale opportunities remain available for further major improvements. Why, again are these equivalents of $50 bills lying on the sidewalk not being picked up? The first, and simplest, answer is that they require upfront investments. This entails obtaining the necessary upfront investment funds and assuming the associated risks. Such risks can be significant, especially given that the costs involved can vary widely. As a result, the main challenge for enabling the global energy efficiency investment market to grow rapidly is to develop more effective systems of financing and risk-sharing. We will discuss these issues in our policy discussion in Chapter 7.

What About Rebound Effects?

There is another major issue regularly raised about energy efficiency investments. If energy-consuming activities can be accomplished at lower costs due to efficiency gains, wouldn't the subsequent fall in energy costs encourage more energy-consuming activities? And to the extent that more energy-consuming economic activity powered specifically by fossil fuels *does* take place because of these efficiency gains, why would improving efficiency help to lower CO_2 emissions? These questions are at the heart of what is termed the "rebound effect."

The possibility that rebound effects could occur was first proposed by William Stanley Jevons in his 1865 book, *The Coal Question*. Jevons argued that the invention of more efficient steam engines would ultimately lead to increased coal consumption, because it would make the use of coal affordable for an increasing number of uses. Overall coal consumption would increase even as the coal used for particular applications may decrease. Jevons wrote, "It is a confusion of ideas to suppose that the economical use of fuel is equivalent to diminished consumption. The very contrary is the truth."

Following from the Jevons's era, research on the extent of rebound effects became the object of significant study in the 1980s and 1990s. Virtually all of the research to date has focused on these effects for advanced economies. What emerges broadly from this literature is that rebound effects do definitely exist. But they also vary substantially, depending on specific circumstances and policy environments.[5]

For example, in the historical period in Britain described by Jevons, the use of steam engines was growing rapidly as a crucial component of the nineteenth-century industrial revolution. The very purpose of producing more efficient steam engines at that time was to facilitate an accelerated rate of industrialization, powered by coal.

But under contemporary conditions in advanced economies, the research finds that, generally speaking, for both automobile travel as well as heating and cooling residences, the rebound effect is likely to lie in the range of 10–30 percent relative to the total amount of energy saved. As an example, consider a driver who switches from driving a Subaru Outback, which averages 29 miles per gallon (mpg), to a Toyota Prius, which gets 50 mpg, with both cars being powered by gasoline. The driver's fuel efficiency will rise by 70 percent by switching to the Prius. But with a rebound effect in the range of 10–30 percent, the driver would drive 7–21 percent more than before. Still, this driver would reduce her emissions between 49 and 63 percent by switching to the Prius.

The rebound effect for home appliances and lighting in advanced economies is weaker, and may be close to zero. A zero rebound effect indicates a saturation point for consumers; utilizing more energy-efficient clothes or dishwashing machines, for example, would likely have little to no impact on how frequently people wash their clothes or dishes. For such activities, when demand for energy services is near its saturation point, efficiency gains will translate proportionally into reduced energy consumption.

The Jevons case has more relevant parallels with many developing countries today, such as China, India, Indonesia, and South Africa. These are expanding economies in which per capita energy consumption is rising. In these cases, we would expect that increased energy efficiency *would* encourage, for example, more intensive use of automobile travel or household appliances. But even in these cases, the *magnitudes* of the rebound effect are likely to be modest in a wide range of cases. For example, in India today, nearly a third of total energy consumption is used for domestic cooking. Not surprisingly, the government's 2006 *Integrated Energy Policy Report* emphasized, that "efficiency of the cooking process should be given a high priority, particularly since this process is currently marked by a poor level of efficiency."[6] Let's assume that India is able to achieve major improvements in the average Indian household's cooking equipment. This is not likely to induce a large increase in cooking and food consumption itself within households.

Significantly lower energy costs in India could, however, lead to substantial increases in automobile travel as well as more energy consumption for heating and cooling buildings. But investing in high-quality public transportation could also offset growing usage of automobiles. In addition, a more egalitarian income distribution would promote relatively more spending on necessities such as efficient cooking equipment and public transportation, and less on higher-end consumption goods, such as air conditioning.

But the more critical consideration here is the historical and policy environment in which efficiency investments are implemented throughout the world. If we consider the case of Britain in the Jevons era, the purpose of improving energy efficiency was precisely to support the greater use of coal-fired power. But in all regions of the global economy in the current era, the overarching purpose of raising energy efficiency quite distinct. The proximate purpose is to maintain or enhance the benefits of energy-driven machines while lowering the need to consume energy to power these machines. The fundamental purpose is, quite simply, to play a major role in stabilizing the global climate.

Thus, for all countries at all levels of development, it is critical that the effort to increase energy efficiency be accompanied by complementary policies that, in combination, will succeed in dramatically reducing CO_2 emissions. One obvious set of complementary measures would be to promote affordable clean renewable energy investments, which would allow for higher levels of energy consumption—including some limited rebound effects—without leading to increases in CO_2 emissions. Another complementary policy would be to discourage fossil fuel consumption through setting a price on carbon emissions. As we discuss in Chapters 4 and 7, this can be accomplished through either a carbon cap or carbon tax. A policy environment that complements energy efficiency investments with strong support for renewable energy and disincentives for fossil fuel consumption will create a much smaller rebound effect than a situation—such as that in Jevons's England—when efficiency was meant to drive industrialization, free of environmental constraints.

The evidence we presented in Table 3.1 on energy intensity levels for different countries is pertinent here. As we saw,

Germany presently operates at an efficiency level roughly 50 percent higher than that of the United States, with the respective intensity ratios at 4.1 versus 6.2 Q-BTUs per $1 trillion in GDP. Brazil is at more than twice the efficiency level of South Korea and nearly three times that of South Africa. There is no evidence that large rebound effects have emerged as a result of the high efficiency standards achieved by Germany and Brazil relative to those of United States, South Korea, and South Africa. Equivalently, there should be no presumption that rebound effects would necessarily be stronger in the United States, South Korea, or South Africa once they began to significantly improve efficiency. The basic determining factor here will be the overall policy environment.

This assessment of the rebound effect has broader resonance. The critical challenge is to create the most effective policy environment for supporting, concurrently, the large-scale expansion of both energy efficiency and clean renewable energy investments as well as the large-scale contraction of the fossil fuel industry.

Producing an abundant supply of clean renewable energy resources is, along with dramatically raising energy efficiency standards, one of the two cornerstones for achieving the IPCC's emissions reduction targets. This means generating energy at rapidly increasing rates for solar, wind, geothermal, clean bioenergy, and small-scale hydro power. Within twenty years, these clean renewable energy sources will need to provide about a third of global energy supply, amounting, in total, to about 150 Q-BTUs.

At present, total renewable sources account for about 13 percent of global energy supply, amounting to about 70 Q-BTUs. However, this 13 percent figure is deceptively high, since high-emissions bioenergy accounts for 10 percent of the total, and large-scale hydro power provides another 2 percent. Wind, solar, and geothermal energy sources combined provide only about 1 percent of global energy supply at present. Thus, hydro, wind, solar, and geothermal power combined provide about 16 Q-BTUs as of 2013. Nevertheless, it is realistic to expect that *clean* renewables—excluding high-emissions bioenergy and with no new large-scale dam projects—could provide close to a third of all global energy resources within twenty years. As of 2013, clean renewable power generation technologies had already added about $200 billion to energy capacity, about 40 percent of new power capacity for all energy sources for 2013.[1]

The main driver here is that the trajectory for prices and costs for renewables is becoming increasingly favorable. Under a wide range of conditions, renewable energy is already at cost parity with non-renewables, or will be so within the next five to ten years. In addition, the price gap that may still exist between fossil fuel energy and clean renewables would close altogether through the establishment of a carbon cap or carbon tax and through elimination of fossil fuel subsidies. As I discuss below, a carbon cap or tax would raise prices for oil, coal, and natural gas relative to renewables. Eliminating fossil fuel subsidies would make clean renewables still more competitive.

It is also important to recognize that the costs for generating clean renewable power will decline sharply as these technologies are increasingly deployed. Regarding solar energy, for example, the International Renewable Energy Agency (IRENA) estimates that costs will fall by as much as 22 percent for every doubling in solar generating capacity.[2] This figure is especially favorable because solar energy currently provides perhaps a quarter of one percent of global energy supply. It is realistic to anticipate that solar energy production will increase between five and tenfold over the next twenty years, which would mean that solar costs could fall 60–80 percent.

At the same time, a major expansion of clean renewable energy production will face major challenges. The most basic question for the viability of clean renewable energy is costs. Can renewable energy really produce energy at costs that are comparable to, or even below, those for non-renewables? We also need to address three additional issues: the impact of bioenergy production and consumption on both emissions and global food prices; the prospects for small-scale hydro power projects, given that large-scale dam construction has serious negative environmental impacts; and the management of solar and wind power intermittency, i.e., the fact that the sun doesn't shine and the wind doesn't blow all day, every day, while the demand for energy persists around-the-clock.

Bioenergy, Emissions, and Food Prices

As noted above, bioenergy presently accounts for about 75 percent of global *renewable* energy supply, which amounts to about 10 percent of total energy supply from all sources. Considering the short- to medium term—within the 20-year time frame on which we are focused in this book—bioenergy will continue to be the largest source of renewable energy in all regions of the globe. For this reason alone, prospects for the bioenergy sector merit careful attention.

Expanding the bioenergy sector clearly raises major concerns. The first is that under currently dominant production methods, consuming bioenergy generates emission levels comparable to those from fossil fuel combustion. We need to understand this point within the framework of the full lifecycle effects on emissions from bioenergy. This full lifecycle includes the burning of wood, ethanol, or agricultural wastes that produce greenhouse gas emissions—CO_2 as well as methane, nitrous oxide, and other greenhouse gases. However, forests and croplands absorb CO_2 through photosynthesis during their growth phases. This period of absorption in the emissions lifecycle generates the "carbon sink" effect associated with bioenergy.

Research estimates vary on the extent to which carbon sinks counterbalance greenhouse gas emissions from bioenergy sources. Two points are critical for our purposes. The first is that the time horizon over which most carbon sinks absorb CO_2 is substantially longer than the time frame over which combustion adds to the supply of greenhouse gas emissions. Consider one major case in point: generating energy from corn ethanol that has been refined through conventional coal-fired processing. According to the U.S. Environmental Protection Agency, over a thirty-year cycle, corn ethanol produced in this way generates emissions levels that are 34 percent *greater* than burning gasoline. But over a hundred-year cycle, net emissions from corn ethanol are roughly comparable to those from gasoline. For our purposes, the thirty-year cycle effects are far more relevant than the hundred-year cycle or beyond, given that we are focused on driving down emissions 40 percent by 2035 and 80 percent by 2050. In addition, these lifecycle effects are influenced by land-use practices associated with the production of bioenergy feedstocks. If, for example, forested areas are converted to agricultural use in order to expand corn production as a bioenergy feedstock, this will consequently reduce the size of the global carbon sink. This is because forests absorb CO_2 much faster than croplands.

The use of agricultural cropland for bioenergy feedstock production raises the second major concern: that this use of cropland will reduce the amount of land devoted to producing food crops, which in turn could reduce global food supply and raise food prices. Any increase in global food prices will have especially adverse effects on low-income people in developing countries, for whom food purchases typically constitute between 50 and 70 percent of overall household budgets.

Global food prices have fluctuated sharply since the early 2000s. In particular, the global food price index rose by 98 percent between 2000 and 2008 after controlling for inflation. This resulted in approximately 130 million additional people experiencing malnutrition. However, the dominant factor explaining this food price spike was not the expansion of agricultural output tied to bioenergy production but rather the rise in speculative financial market activity on the commodities futures market. This becomes clear through recognizing that, during this food price spike, other commodities besides food experienced similar sharp price increases, including metals such as copper, aluminum, lead, and nickel that have no direct connection to the production of food crops or bioenergy.

The development of a clean bioenergy sector can address concerns about both climate stabilization and food security. Droughts, floods, and other extreme weather events have themselves been major factors contributing to food price spikes. In addition, any possible impacts of expanding bioenergy production on food prices can be minimized through encouraging investments that both raise agricultural productivity and expand the use of non-food agricultural resources—such as switchgrass, corn stover, and waste grease—as the raw material feedstocks for bioenergy.[3] Through using these non-foodcrops as feedstocks, and through utilizing renewable energy sources for refining these raw materials as needed, bioenergy can provide energy while generating no net increases in CO_2 emissions.

Building the bioenergy sector needs to be based, then, on low- to zero-emissions sources, i.e. "clean" bioenergy. To date, the global production of clean bioenergy is negligible. However, within the European Union, Germany has taken a strong lead in advancing regulations that would phase out bioenergy generated with food crops and support the rapid development of clean bioenergy production.

Large- vs. Small-Scale Hydro Power

Hydro power is the other renewable energy source currently operating at major production levels in various regions of the globe. As noted above, hydro power provides about 2 percent of all global energy supply. But virtually all of this hydro power is generated by large-scale dam projects. But these projects produce major negative effects on regional ecosystems and communities. The Three Gorges Dam in China, the world's largest power station, is the most obvious case in point. The construction of the dam between 1994 and 2008 led to the displacement of 1.3 million people, along with the flooding of 13 cities, over 100 towns, and 1,000 villages. The dam has also produced a range of negative environmental impacts, including deforestation, loss of biodiversity and sedimentary erosion in the reservoir, which in turn led to major landslides.

Prospects are much more favorable for small-scale hydro. These are projects that operate in rivers and streams without requiring the construction of a dam or reservoir. Small-scale hydro projects utilize a conduit running parallel to the flow of a stream or river, which carries the water to a turbine placed within the river or stream. Once the water flows through the turbine to generate electricity, it is returned to its natural flow. As summarized by Lea Kosnick, a researcher focusing on the economics of small-scale hydro development, "Such small generation facilities have very few of the negative riverine impacts to which larger, more conventional hydropower plants have been prone."[4]

As a case in point, the prospects in India for both large- and small-scale hydro development are instructive. It has long been documented that the construction and subsequent operation of large-scale dams in India have had serious negative impacts on the nearby communities and environment. This has emerged most recently in struggles over the construction of what would be the largest dam in India, the Lower Subansiri Dam in Northeast India. Construction of the project has been stalled for three years because of massive protests by local people and the regional farmers' organization.

By contrast, small-scale hydro projects are widely seen—at least potentially—as much more ecologically viable. A recent World Bank assessment concluded that small-scale hydro is a "very attractive" but still "largely untapped" resource for India, especially in the states of Himachal Pradesh, Jammu and Kashmir, and Uttarakhand. According to the World Bank study, these states "have 65 percent of India's small hydropower resource and among the lowest generation costs."[5]

Nevertheless, a 2014 study by Mark Baker on all 49 completed small-scale hydro projects in the Northern India state of Himachal Pradesh still found that the vast majority of these projects "have generated unmitigated negative effects, ranging from disruptions to local irrigation systems and water-powered mills, to the undermining of fisheries-based livelihoods."[6] Baker does not dismiss the potential opportunities for small-scale hydro in India outright. He rather suggests the development of alternative institutional arrangements that would establish the needs of local communities and ecologies a central place in the planning process. Baker recognizes that it is possible with small-scale hydro to protect local communities and ecologies. He does not think this is, in any way, a realistic prospect with large-scale dam projects.

Intermittency with Solar and Wind Power

Solar and wind cannot generate energy continuously, unlike fossil fuel, nuclear, bioenergy, and hydro power. Wind power depends on when and how intensively the wind is blowing, while solar energy depends on the amount of daylight and the extent of cloud cover.

But intermittency should not present major difficulties as the clean renewable energy sectors develop throughout the global economy. The key is to develop solar and wind within integrated energy systems, as opposed to isolated, standalone resources. An integrated energy system could entail, for example, relying on wind power to a greater extent at night when the wind is more frequently plentiful, while solar power provides the primary energy supply during daylight hours. It will also entail using the non-intermittent renewable sources— clean bioenergy, hydro, and geothermal power—as baselines to produce continuous energy, regardless of the specific ways in which solar and wind supply might vary. We should also expect that storage capacity with solar and wind power will advance as part of the overall technological development of these sectors.

Finally, the clean energy transition framework I am proposing still anticipates that oil, coal, natural gas and nuclear power will supply no less than two-thirds of all energy supply over the next twenty years. Non-renewable energy sources, in other words, will remain available in abundance to contribute to the global energy supply baseload. This will provide a more than adequate time frame for resolving the challenges that will emerge as a result of solar and wind power intermittency.

Renewable Energy Costs

Renewable energy costs vary widely depending on technologies, feedstocks, available resources, and the specific conditions at any given power-generating site. Table 4.1 below, based on figures from IRENA's 2013 study, provides a clear picture of cost ranges for generating electricity from renewables for 2012 and 2020 in all regions of the world. The data are presented as cents per kilowatt hour of electricity supply. The 2012 figures are based on IRENA's survey of actual renewable production activity. The 2020 figures reflect IRENA's estimates as to how effectively new renewable technologies will be adapted throughout the world in the immediate coming years.

Table 4.1 Costs of Generating Electricity from Alternative Energy Sources
Figures are U.S. cents per kilowatt hour (kWh)

	2012	2020
Fossil Fuels in Advanced Economics	7 – 11	7 - 11
Biomass	5 – 22	5 – 17
Hydro	3 – 12	3 – 12
Wind—onshore	7 – 12	7 – 11
Solar—photovoltaics (PV)	11 – 36	9 – 32
Geothermal	3 – 11	3 – 11

Source: IRENA (2013)

These cost figures include three major components: capital costs of building new productive equipment, the operations and maintenance costs of generating electricity, and the costs of transmitting electricity through the grid. It is important to recognize that, in many situations with renewable energy, transmission costs can be minimized, or even eliminated altogether, with small-scale projects. Prime examples here are individual rooftop solar units and community-based wind farms through which energy is supplied on the spot or without having to rely on large-scale electrical grid systems. I return to this point in Chapter 7, where I consider alternative forms of ownership that will emerge with the advance of clean energy technologies.

From Table 4.1, we see that, as of 2012, the midpoint costs of generating electricity through biomass, hydro, onshore wind, and geothermal power are all at rough parity with fossil fuel costs in advanced economies. Fossil fuel costs ranged between 7 and 11 cents per kilowatt hour (kWh). With biomass, the lower-end costs at 5 cents per kWh are less than those for fossil fuels, while the high-end costs, at 22 cents per kWh, are much higher. With hydro power, the low-end costs are also lower than fossil fuels, at 3 cents per kWh, while the higher-end costs are still roughly the same as fossil fuels. The differences are comparable for wind and geothermal power. IRENA estimates that these cost differences will narrow by 2020. Solar energy is the only renewable source where the cost range is significantly higher than for fossil fuels. As we also see in Table 4.1, IRENA estimates that this will still remain true as of 2020. Nevertheless, as we have discussed before, if investments in solar capacity continue to expand rapidly, costs are likely to decline well below IRENA's estimates.

These highly favorable prospects for renewable energy costs are consistent with recent market developments. For example, the *2013 Sustainable Energy in America Factbook* published by Bloomberg New Energy Finance and the Business Council for Sustainable Energy reported that:

> The . . . costs of electricity for renewable technologies have plummeted. For example, the costs of electricity generated by average solar power plants has fallen from 31 cents per kilowatt hour in 2009 to 14 cents per kilowatt hour in 2012, according to our global benchmarking analysis based on already financed projects from around the world. These figures exclude the effect of tax credits and other incentives, which would bring these costs down even lower.[7]

As of August 2013, this declining price trajectory for solar and accompanying recent growth surge in the industry prompted Jon Wellinghoff, then Chair of the U.S. Federal Energy Regulatory Commission (FERC), to assert that "Solar is growing so fast it is going to overtake everything. . . . At its present growth rate, solar will overtake wind in about 10 years. It is going to be the dominant player. Everybody's roof is out there."[8]

The cost competitiveness of clean renewable energy sources relative to fossil fuels would improve still further if the fossil fuel industry were no longer supported by public subsidies and were instead forced to bear the costs of negative environmental impacts. At present, the lower average costs and narrower cost range for fossil fuels reflects the fact that these sectors are operating with mature technologies that have been developed over decades and have been supported on a massive global scale over this full period by both private investors and public subsidies.

How large are fossil fuel subsidies? The International Energy Agency provides estimates as to the extent of consumption subsidies only for fossil fuels—i.e. when governments set the sale price to consumers for fossil fuel products lower than the market price and cover the difference through public funds. The IEA reported that, as of 2013, forty countries provided consumption subsidies, which amounted to a total of $548 billion, equaling about 5 percent of GDP, on average. For many of these countries, this subsidy is higher than the level of spending on education or health. The IEA estimates that the $548 billion in total consumption subsidies amounted to 23 percent of the sale price of fossil fuels—that is, on average, fossil fuel prices would be 23 percent higher throughout the globe if there were no government subsidies. The overall figure would be higher still if production-based subsidies were included along with consumption subsidies. Estimates of these additional subsidies range widely, between an additional $100 and $400 billion. Production-level subsidies are hard to measure because public reporting on them is highly uneven.

Governments defend their ongoing use of fossil fuel subsidies based on three major factors: holding down the costs of energy for low-income households; promoting economic growth and jobs through maintaining low energy prices; and, for fossil-fuel producing countries, promoting their domestic industry and correspondingly reducing oil import dependency. In fact, policymakers could achieve all of these basic objectives through alternative measures that would be much more productive, starting with committing their economies to a large-scale clean energy investment program that would deliver affordable energy and expand domestic job opportunities. The subsidies are highly ineffective even strictly as a means of supporting low-income households. A study by the IEA found that "a large share—if not the bulk—of the subsidies aimed at helping the poor often ends up going to higher income households, as they can afford to consume more of the subsidized fuels—aggravating the very inequality they are meant to reduce."[9]

Policies for the fossil fuel industry should be moving in exactly the opposite direction —that is, to incorporate into fossil fuel prices the environmental damage caused by burning oil, coal and natural gas. The two most widely recognized ways of doing so are carbon taxes and carbon caps. A carbon cap establishes a firm limit on the allowable level of emissions for major polluting entities, such as utilities, and would raise fossil fuel prices by limiting their supply. A carbon tax, on the other hand, would raise fossil fuel prices directly.

One widely discussed approach—for example, one developed by the U.S. Energy Department—would aim to phase in a price of $75 per ton of CO_2 emissions, through either a tax or a cap. The impact of this price increase would vary considerably between oil, coal and natural gas, because the CO_2 content varies between them relative to their market prices. The final impact on market prices would also depend on the specific conditions in energy markets at any given time. But as a rough approximation, the $75 per ton price would likely mean that coal prices would more than double, natural gas prices would rise by about 60 percent, and oil prices would rise by about 20 percent. In general, the effect would be to make all renewable energy sources other than solar cheaper than fossil fuels under most circumstances. Solar itself would become cost competitive with coal and natural gas in most situations. These relative gains in competitiveness for clean renewables would be in addition to those achieved through eliminating fossil fuel subsidies.

Of course, in practice, establishing a carbon price on fossil fuel supplies and eliminating subsidies would need to be implemented incrementally to provide ample lead-time for countries to adjust to higher prices. In particular, careful attention would need to be paid to the fact that higher fossil fuel prices would impact the living standards of low-income households much more than the affluent because energy costs absorb a much higher share of lower-income households' consumption. We take up these considerations in Chapter 7. For now, the critical point is that the costs of most clean renewables are currently at rough parity or within reach of fossil fuels under a wide range of settings. These costs would become lower than those for fossil fuels if we incorporated some version of carbon pricing and eliminated fossil fuel subsidies.

How Costly to Expand Renewable Energy Capacity?

As noted above, the overall cost figures in Table 4.1 incorporate the investment costs of building new renewable energy productive equipment. Examples include the costs of building solar panels and wind turbines and installing them, creating new small-scale hydro power operations, and producing the equipment to refine switchgrass into bioenergy. It is critical for our discussion that we consider these particular costs on their own, since they will be the basis on which we can estimate how much total clean renewable energy capacity can expand through new investments. Estimates of these capital costs vary widely, based on the specific energy system being newly constructed as well as the specific setting for such new energy operations.

The most detailed data available come from the U.S. Energy Department. These estimates for the United States assume that costs will decline steadily over time as higher levels of clean renewable capital investments encourage innovation. Working from these U.S. figures, we can get a rough cost approximation for a combined set of investments over 2016–35 to produce the equipment needed to expand production in clean bioenergy, small-scale hydro, wind, solar, and geothermal power by one Q-BTU. The rough figure I derive from the Department of Energy statistics is $230 billion per Q-BTU (see Appendix 1 for details).

How does this U.S.-based investment cost figure correspond with investment costs in the rest of the world? In most of the world, average labor costs will be far below those in the United States. For example, average manufacturing labor costs in Brazil are about a third of those in the United States; in China they are only 5 percent, and in India they are only 3 percent. At the same time, *other* costs involved in producing capital equipment—including materials, transportation, administration, and energy costs—are likely to be equivalent to, if not higher than, those in the United States. Overall then, it is reasonable to work with a rough figure that, as a global average over 2016–35, the costs of expanding clean energy productive capacity by one Q-BTU will be about $200 billion.

Working with this figure, let us return to the framework we discussed in Chapter 1: to achieve the IPCC's 40 percent emission reduction target, the global economy will need to be producing about 150 Q-BTUs of clean renewable energy by 2035. The 2012 total production level of clean renewables was about 16 Q-BTUs. This means that we will need to increase clean renewable production nine-fold. This amounts to an average growth rate of about 11 percent per year. At an average of $200 billion per Q-BTU of capacity, this means that the overall costs will be about $24 trillion, or $1.2 trillion per year for twenty years.

In working with this rough average cost figure, it is important to emphasize again a point I made in Chapter 3 about energy efficiency cost estimates. It is less important to establish accurate cost estimates for any given country, with any of the alternative clean renewable energy sources, than to evaluate the viability of large-scale renewable estimates when we assume costs will be relatively high. If the actual costs of expanding renewable capacity end up being significantly lower than U.S. costs in countries such as India, China, Indonesia, Brazil, or for that matter, Germany, South Korea of Spain, the viability of the project to rapidly expand clean renewables on a global scale is only strengthened.

Getting from Here to There

In Chapter 5, I will work through some details as to how this level of investment could be realistically sustained, along with large-scale investment in energy efficiency. For now, I will focus on the clean renewable sector itself. From the full range of evidence we have reviewed in this chapter, we can conclude that, in all regions of the world, there is almost certainly some combination of clean renewable sources that can produce significant energy supplies at cost parity relative to non-renewables, either at present or within the next five years.

Consider again the case of India. According to the data provided by IRENA, in some parts of India, clean bioenergy could be supplied for as low as 1–2 cents per kWh to produce electricity. By contrast, the average cost of fossil fuels is between 7 and 11 cents kWh, without taking account of carbon pricing. However, this cheap supply of clean bioenergy will be limited by the amount of switchgrass, corn stover, or waste grease that can be provided without creating serious strain on India's agricultural resources for food production. But India could turn to small-scale hydro production in regions of the country where, as we saw, a recent World Bank study found that these resources are "very attractive" but "largely untapped." Costs in these regions could be as low as 2 cents per kWh. India could next maximize its low-cost wind power capacity: IRENA estimates these costs to be around 3 cents per kWh, compared to an average cost of 8 cents. India could then turn to solar power, where the low-end cost is 8 cents compared to a much higher average of 23 cents. India could incorporate more and more solar power into its overall energy mix as these costs come down with greater usage.

As this example suggests, which particular combination of clean renewable sources can be utilized most efficiently depends on context. Moreover, establishing the point at which any given clean renewable resource can effectively substitute *at scale* for non-renewables will also depend on the specific resources available and broader economic circumstances within a specific region. As such, on-the-ground decision makers—including community organizations, social movements, government policymakers, and private investors—will have to examine all the relevant considerations as they work to build viable clean energy systems within their own regions of the globe.

5 How to Hit the CO_2 Emissions Reduction Target

This chapter presents my approach for a twenty-year global clean energy investment project. The basic idea is simple: we increase global investments into energy efficiency and clean renewable energy by 1.5 percent of GDP relative to the IEA's business-as-usual (BAU) scenario for 2035.[1] In all, then, my framework assumes that 1.7–1.8 percent of global GDP will be channeled into clean energy investments on an annual basis.

If these investments are made, we can reach the 2035 emissions reduction target of 20 billion tons of CO_2, or 2.3 tons of emissions per person. This is a stark alternative to the grim prospect of the IEA's BAU forecast that 2035 global CO_2 emissions will be at 43.3 billion tons, or 5.0 tons per person.

Of course, my approach involves making future projections. All such economic forecasting exercises are fraught with pitfalls and prone to error. The late U.S. economist Ezra Solomon once remarked that "the only function of economic forecasting is to make astrology look respectable."[2] Nevertheless, if we are going to have a chance at stabilizing the climate, we need to understand as best we can what level of clean energy investments will be needed and how quickly these investments need to be made to achieve gains in energy efficiency and expansions in clean renewable energy supply. We have no choice but to work as carefully as possible with some basic economic forecasting tools.

All economic forecasts are based on assumptions about what we think will happen in the future: for example, how much we think global GDP is likely to expand over the next twenty years and the impact on CO$_2$ emissions of this level of growth. We then combine our chosen assumptions into a fuller picture as to how economic activity over the globe is likely to proceed over time. If the assumptions are not realistic, the forecast will be unreliable. But the real world is also full of idiosyncrasies that are difficult to recognize, much less adequately capture in a model. In short, the world is complicated. I am perfectly willing to acknowledge that I do not know about, much less understand all the complications that could be relevant for the matter at hand. But even if I did understand all such complications, I could not possibly incorporate all of them into a forecasting model. The more complications we incorporate, the greater the likelihood that some of them will be wrong. This too will lead to unreliable projections.

My approach is to see what happens on the basis of a very small number of realistic assumptions. The purely technical aspects of the model can be readily reproduced by any reasonably competent high school student, working only with a pencil, paper and perhaps a cheap smart phone calculator. I go through the technical steps of the model in Appendix 2.

The main assumptions of the model are as follows:

- *Global GDP growth trend.* All IEA models assume an average global GDP growth of 3.4 percent per year between 2012 and 2040. My model incorporates this figure.

- *Clean energy investments as share of global GDP.* I assume that investments in energy efficiency and clean renewables will increase by 1.5 percent of GDP over the level that is built into the IEA's BAU model. As noted above, the IEA does not make clear what they have assumed for clean energy and energy efficiency investments as a share of global GDP.
- *Average costs for increasing energy efficiency and expanding clean renewable production.* I assume that the average costs to increase energy efficiency by 1 Q-BTU will be $30 billion. I also assume that the average costs to expand productive capacity of clean renewable energy by 1 Q-BTU will be $200 billion. Both of these average cost estimates derive from the discussions in Chapters 3 and 4. The energy efficiency cost figure, in particular, is well on the high end of the figures we reviewed there.
- *Three-year delay in bringing the project to scale.* This is a twenty-year investment project. But given that the current level of clean energy investments is in the range of 0.2–0.3 percent of global GDP, we must allow some time to pass before we can expect investments to rise by 1.5 percent of annual GDP. To reflect this consideration, I assume that it will require three years of major effort to raise global clean energy investments by 1.5 percent of GDP relative to the IEA's BAU scenario. We therefore assume that the 1.5 percent of GDP increase in global investments will occur over seventeen years within the full twenty-year investment cycle. The initial three years will be needed to develop an adequate policy and financing environment to sustain clean energy investments at this level.

- *Limited role for nuclear energy.* In recognizing the major public safety concerns with nuclear energy, I assume that global nuclear energy capacity will remain at its 2012 level of 25 Q-BTUs. This contrasts with the IEA's BAU assumption that nuclear energy production will rise by 60 percent, to 40 Q-BTUs by 2035.

Results

The results of the model are summarized in Table 5.1 and Figures 5.1–5.3 (pp. 66–68). Starting from the 2012 data, the table and figures compare my forecast to the IEA's BAU model.

Beginning with Table 5.1, total global energy consumption in 2035 falls from 754 Q-BTUs under the IEA framework to 444 Q-BTUs under my model, a decline of 41 percent in total consumption. This results from annual investments of 0.5 percent of global GDP greater than the IEA's BAU framework, yielding 310 Q-BTUs in energy efficiency savings relative to the IEA BAU model.

In addition, clean renewables production increases by 93.5 Q-BTUs in 2035, over and above the IEA's estimate of 40 Q-BTUs, an increase of 134 percent. This results from annual investments in clean renewables of 1 percent of global GDP greater than the IEA's model.

The net result of rising efficiency, greater clean energy capacity, and a fixed level of nuclear energy yields a total demand for fossil fuel energy and high-emissions renewables of 286 Q-BTUs. This is a 63 percent decline relative to the 764 Q-BTU figure from the IEA's BAU scenario.

The final two rows of Table 5.1 show what this means in terms of global energy emissions. Under the IEA's BAU case, total CO$_2$ emissions are at 43.3 billion tons, or 5.0 tons per capita, while

Table 5.1 Impact of 20-year Clean Energy Investment Program Relative to International Energy Agency's BAU Scenario for 2035

	IEA BAU Scenario (IEA 2014)	20-year Clean Energy Investment Scenario *(= 1.5% of GDP clean energy investment increase over IEA-BAU)*	Difference between IEA-BAU and Clean Energy Investment Scenarios
Total Energy Consumption In Q-BTUs	754 Q- BTUs	444 Q- BTUs *(= 754 – 310 BTUs in energy efficiency savings)*	-41%
Total Clean Renewable Energy Supply	40 Q- BTUs *(5.3% of supply)*	133.5 Q- BTUs *(= 40 + 93.5-BTUs through renewable energy investments) (30.1% of supply)*	+134%
Total Nuclear Power Supply	40 Q-BTUs *(5.3% of supply)*	25 Q-BTUs *(5.6% of supply)*	-25%
Total Fossil Fuel + High-Emissions Renewables	674 Q- BTUs *(89.4% of supply)*	286 Q-BTUs *(= 444 Q-BTUs total consumption – 133.5 from renewables + 25 from nuclear) (64.4% of supply)*	-63%
Total CO_2 Emissions *(metric tons)*	43.3 billion tons	20 billion tons *(= 286 Q-BTUs x .07 billion tons/Q-BTU*	-54%
Total CO_2 Emissions per capita *(with global population = 8.7 billion)*	5.0	2.3	-54%

Sources: See Chapter 5 text and Appendix 2.

Figure 5.1 Total global energy consumption under alternative scenarios, measured in Q-BTUs.

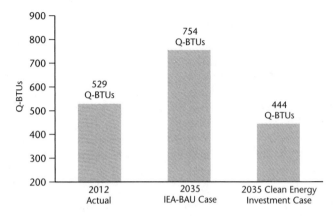

Sources: EIA, International Energy Statistics; IEA 2014.

Figure 5.2 Fossil fuel energy consumption under alternative scenarios, measured in Q-BTUs.

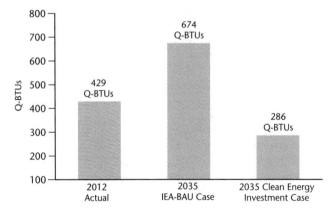

Sources: EIA, International Energy Statistics; IEA 2014.

Figure 5.3 Global CO_2 emissions under alternative scenarios.

A) Total Global Emissions

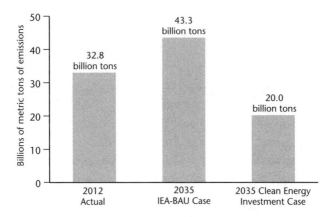

B) Global Emissions Per Capita

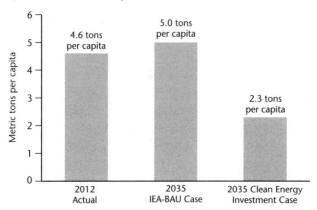

Sources: IEA 2014; Table 5.1.

under my model, global emissions fall to 20 billion tons by 2035, which amounts to 2.3 tons per person globally. In short, global CO_2 emissions fall by 54 percent relative to the IEA's estimate.

These contrasts are displayed even more clearly in Figures 5.1– 5.3. Figure 5.1 shows total global energy consumption in 2012 along with the projected 2035 figures. Under the IEA case, total consumption rises by 43 percent, from 529 to 754 Q-BTUs while in my model it falls by 16 percent, from 529 to 444 Q-BTUs.

In Figure 5.2, we see a similar pattern with respect to fossil fuel energy consumption only. Under the IEA's BAU case, fossil fuel consumption rises between 2012 and 2035 by 57 percent, from 429 to 674 Q-BTUs while under my model it falls from 429 to 286 Q-BTUs, a 33 percent decline. The upper panel of Figure 5.3 shows that global CO_2 emissions were at 32.7 billion tons in 2012. Under the IEA's BAU scenario, emissions rise to 43.3 tons, an increase of 32 percent. Through following this scenario, climate stabilization within the next fifty years would be a near impossibility, assuming the IPCC's analysis is even roughly accurate. By contrast, under the clean energy investment scenario I have presented here, global CO_2 emissions fall to 20 billion tons as of 2035, a 39 percent decline—that is, a decline that would basically meet the IPCC's standard of a 40 percent reduction.

The lower panel of Figure 5.3 shows these same results expressed in terms of per capita emissions. As we see, global emissions were at 4.6 tons per capita in 2012. They would rise to 5.0 tons per capita under the IEA's BAU scenario but fall to 2.3 tons per capita under the clean energy investment scenario I have presented. Reducing global emissions to 2.3 tons per capita would put the global economy onto a long-term trajectory through which, according to the IPCC, climate stabilization can become a reality.

Country-Specific Emissions Reductions

In Table 5.2, I show country-specific per capita emissions levels for major, and highly diverse, economies—Brazil, China, India, Indonesia, Germany, South Africa, South Korea, Spain and the United States. These country-specific estimates are developed within the framework of the global 1.5 percent of GDP investment increase.[3] As the top row of Table 5.2 shows, the reduction in global per capita emissions is, again, 54 percent. Among the nine countries we have included here, the range in emissions reductions is between the low of 30 percent for South Africa and the high of 62 percent for Spain. There are several factors at play generating these differences.

Table 5.2 Emissions Per Capita through IEA-BAU Scenario and Clean Energy Investment Program for 2035

	IEA 2035 BAU Scenario (IEA 2104)	20-year Clean Energy Investment Scenario	Emissions Reduction difference between Scenarios
GLOBAL	5.0	2.3	-54%
Brazil	3.3	1.5	-55%
China	5.6	2.6	-54%
India	3.1	2.1	-32%
Indonesia	7.9	3.6	-54%
Germany	8.9	4.9	-45%
South Africa	16.4	11.4	-30%
South Korea	13.3	6.7	-50%
Spain	6.9	2.6	-62%
United States	14.4	5.8	-60%

Sources: See Appendix 2.

For example, for South Africa, the economy at present is heavily dependent on coal as its primary energy source. Even after allowing for a major retrenchment in its coal sector, the country will still be relying on coal to a substantial extent as of 2035. In addition, at present, the South African economy is also among the least efficient in the world in its use of energy. So here again, even with incorporating major improvements in efficiency, South Africa will remain inefficient relative to the global average.

By contrast, Spain already is a relatively strong green economy performer, both in terms of its level of energy efficiency and its reliance on clean energy sources. As of March 2015, 47 percent of the country's electricity was generated from clean renewable sources, mainly wind power but with a small solar energy sector that has been growing as well. Spain's GDP is also relatively high, at roughly $30,000 per capita as of 2014. If we assume that Spain can sustain a positive growth trajectory over the next 20 years off of this high GDP level, this growth will, in turn, generate a large pool of investment funds to further expand its clean energy sectors and drive its fossil fuel consumption to less than 40 percent of the country's total energy supply (while also allowing its nuclear energy sector to shut down entirely).

For the case of India, the per capita emissions reduction is relatively low because the country is presently operating at a very low energy consumption level. Rapid economic growth will generate large increases in the demand for energy services. Under this situation, the fact that the country can still generate a sharp decline in per capita emissions would be a major achievement.

Indonesia is aiming to emulate India and China, by moving onto a rapid economic growth trajectory over the next 20 years. The government's own business-as-usual model incorporates virtually no provisions for CO_2 emissions reductions. Thus, in this case, channeling 1.5 percent of Indonesia's rapidly growing GDP into clean energy investments will yield a major 54 percent reduction in per capita emissions, equal to the average global emissions reduction level.

China and the U.S. are the two largest countries in terms of both energy consumption and CO_2 emissions, as well as GDP. China's reduction, like that for Indonesia, would be equal to the global average at 54 percent. This would bring China's emissions level to 2.6 tons per capita, which is only modestly above the global target figure of 2.3 tons per capita. For China to get to 2.6 tons per capita would be a huge accomplishment.

At 5.8 tons per capita as of 2035, the U.S. would still be more than twice as high as the global target of 2.3 tons. However, the 60 percent decline in per capita emissions in the U.S. would also represent a tremendous advance toward reaching the global target figure.

Would it be fair, as of 2035, for the people living in the U.S. to continue to emit more than twice the global per capita emissions figure? We raised the issue of fairness in Chapter 1 and will return to it in Chapter 8. For now, the critical finding of my model is that, through investing between 1.5–2 percent of global GDP per year in energy efficiency and clean renewable energy sources, we can chart a realistic path to achieve the IPCC's reduction target. This result provides a valuable framework for considering what constitutes fairness within this or any other climate stabilization agenda.

6 Expanding Job Opportunities through Clean Energy Investments

The massive investments in energy efficiency and clean renewable energy necessary to stabilize the climate will also drive job expansion, in all regions of the world, for countries at all levels of development. Yet there is a widely held view that protecting the environment and expanding job opportunities are necessarily in conflict, creating severe and unavoidable trade-offs. How can there be such huge differences in perspective over a question that is subject to verification through the consideration of evidence?

Aside from posturing by fossil fuel industry spokespeople or pure ideologues, two serious issues contribute to the confusion. The first is that all modern economies, regardless of their current level of development, need an abundance of affordable energy in order to grow at healthy rates, and thereby expand job opportunities. Limiting the supply or raising the price of oil, coal, and natural gas would, by definition, make fossil fuel energy more scarce and costly. Employment opportunities would then have to fall, according to this logic.

But as we have seen in Chapter 5, the full energy mix resulting from twenty years of investments will include roughly 30 percent from clean renewables after efficiency standards have dramatically increased. The evidence we have reviewed in Chapters 3 and 4 show that there is no reason to expect that energy prices would have to rise under this scenario, given that investments in energy efficiency will generate savings on energy costs and that most clean renewable energy prices will be at rough parity or lower than those from fossil fuels and nuclear power.

The second issue is that building a clean energy economy, and bringing down global emissions to 20 billion tons (2.3 tons per capita), will be bad for *fossil fuel industry* jobs specifically. In the United States, for example, this position has been advanced aggressively regarding the Keystone pipeline project: building and maintaining the Keystone pipeline from the Canadian border through the Midwest to Louisiana would create jobs, while preventing the project means that these jobs will never exist.

This second argument is true, as far as it goes. There is absolutely no way to reduce global fossil fuel production by 40 percent within twenty years, or by 80 percent within thirty-five years, without also cutting employment in the fossil fuel industry by roughly proportional amounts. That can only mean far fewer jobs for coal miners, oil rig operators, and natural gas delivery truck drivers.

But what this perspective leaves out is that, overall, building a clean energy economy will be a positive source of *net job creation* in all regions of the globe, even after we take account of the job losses generated by fossil fuel industry retrenchments. This conclusion is supported by work my co-authors and I have done on job creation through spending within both the clean energy and fossil fuel sectors within various countries. We have studied this question for a diverse set of nine major economies: Brazil, China, India, Indonesia, Germany, South Africa, South Korea, Spain and the United States. (We are continuing this work for other countries as well.) We have found that building a clean energy economy will be a positive source of job creation in all of these countries, despite substantial differences in labor markets and energy infrastructures.

Tables 6.1 (p. 79) and 6.2 (p. 81) present the main findings of our work. Table 6.1 shows the number of jobs that will be generated in each country through spending $1 million on either building a new clean energy economy or maintaining the country's existing fossil-fuel based energy infrastructure. Table 6.2 gives the same estimates for spending 1.5 percent of current-level GDP. That is, the data in Table 6.2 simply takes the figures from Table 6.1 and scales the level of spending to 1.5 percent of each country's GDP as opposed to spending a flat $1 million on clean energy in each country.

Where the Data Come From

Our estimates draw directly from national surveys of public and private economic enterprises within each country. These data are organized systematically within national "input-output" statistical tables for each country's economy. Here is one specific example of our methodology. If a business invests an additional $1 million on energy efficiency retrofits of an existing building, we are able to measure, using the input-output tables, how much of the $1 million the business will spend on paying wages and benefits to workers and on needed supplies (such as windows, insulation, and lumber), how much will be left over to keep as profits, and how many new workers will be hired by the window, insulation, and lumber companies as a result. We also examine this same set of questions for investment projects in renewable energy as well as spending on operations within the fossil-fuel energy sectors.[1]

Dividing Countries between Fossil Fuel Producers and Importers

I have divided our full set of nine countries into two groups in Tables 6.1 and 6.2. The first group includes countries that are, at present, large-scale producers of either oil, coal or natural gas, or some combination of all three. The second group includes countries that are heavily dependent on imports for their fossil fuel supplies. This distinction is crucial for assessing the impact on job opportunities within each country through advancing a clean energy transition. That is, with countries that are large-scale fossil fuel producers, we have to allow that the shift away from fossil fuels to clean renewables and energy efficiency will also entail a significant decline in employment opportunities in these countries' fossil fuel industries. For this set of countries—Brazil, China, India, Indonesia, South Africa and the United States—I am assuming for our discussion that a 1.5 percent of GDP increase in clean energy investments in the countries is equally matched by a 1.5 percent of GDP decline in spending on fossil fuel production. Thus, net job creation occurs in these countries through their clean energy investment project only when spending a given amount of money on clean energy investments creates more jobs within the country than spending the same amount of money on fossil fuel production.

In the United States, for example, if clean energy investments and fossil fuel production both generate 10 jobs per $1 million in spending, then shifting $1 million out of fossil fuel production and into clean energy investments will produce no net gains in jobs at all. In fact, for the U.S., as we see in Table 6.1, spending $1 million on clean energy investments generate, on average, 8.7 jobs while fossil fuel production generates 3.7 jobs. Shifting energy-sector spending from fossil fuels to clean energy therefore produces an average of 5 new jobs per $1 million in spending within the U.S. economy. The upper panel of Table 6.1 reports the figures for the U.S. and the other fossil-fuel producing economies. The upper panel of Table 6.2 then shows the net gains in job creation for the fossil-fuel producing countries from shifting 1.5 percent of GDP into clean energy production and out of fossil-fuel production.

In our second, smaller group of fossil-fuel importing countries—Germany, South Korea, and Spain—the jobs generated by investing 1.5 percent of GDP in clean energy is not counteracted by an equivalent shift out of domestic spending on fossil fuel production, but rather only a decline in fossil fuel imports. In the lower panel of Table 6.1, I therefore show for Germany, South Korea and Spain the figures for job creation through clean energy investments, without also reporting figures on job created by fossil fuel production. In the lower panel of Table 6.2, I then show job creation in each of these economies through channeling 1.5 percent of GDP on clean energy investments.[2]

Beyond these specific issues on job creation, it is important to recognize, more generally, that the heavy fossil fuel importing countries will enjoy greater proportional benefits through their clean energy investment programs: first, these countries produce jobs through their clean energy investments without facing counteracting fossil fuel sector job losses; and, second, equally critically, they reduce their dependency on imported energy sources. In the next chapter, I consider the benefits for Germany, South Korea and Spain, and other heavy oil importers of reducing their oil import dependency. We focus on job creation effects in our present discussion.

Job Creation Estimates by Country

As we see in Table 6.1, the number of jobs created through spending within the energy industry varies widely by country. For example, among the six fossil-fuel producing countries, we see that investing $1 million on clean energy investments generates about 9 jobs in the United States, 37 jobs in Brazil, 71 jobs in South Africa, 133 jobs in China, and 262 jobs in India. For the three fossil fuel importing countries, clean energy investments generate about 10 jobs in Germany, 13 jobs in Spain, and 15 jobs in South Korea.

These differences are driven mainly by the wide range of average wage levels. For example, as of 2010, average manufacturing wages were about $1.50 in India, $11 in Brazil, and $44 in Germany. Such differences need to be kept in mind. But our main interest is with the relative job creation figures *within each of the countries*. This is especially the case for the fossil-fuel producing countries, in which we need to counterbalance job gains from clean energy investments against job losses through declining spending within domestic fossil fuel industries.

We see in the upper panel of Table 6.1 that in all six fossil fuel producing countries, investing in clean energy generates more jobs per $1 million in spending than channeling that same amount of money into each country's fossil fuel industry. In most cases, the net increase in job creation is substantial. The largest difference is in Indonesia, where clean energy

Table 6.1 Jobs Generated through Spending $1 Million on Clean Energy versus Fossil Fuel Production

Large-scale Fossil Fuel Producing Countries

	Clean Energy Jobs per $1 million	Fossil Fuel Jobs per $1 million	Job Increase through Clean Energy Spending relative to Fossil Fuels
Brazil	37.1	21.2	+75%
China	133.1	74.4	+79%
India	261.9	129.1	+103%
Indonesia	99.1	22.0	+350%
South Africa	70.6	33.1	+113%
United States	8.7	3.7	+135%

Large-scale Fossil-Fuel Importing Countries

	Clean Energy Jobs per $1 million
Germany	9.7
South Korea	14.6
Spain	13.4

Sources: See Pollin et al. (2015a) Chapter 6 and Appendix 2 for estimating methodology.

investments generate 99 jobs per $1 million, while spending on fossil fuels produces only 22—a difference of 350 percent. In Brazil, China, South Africa, and the United States, clean energy investments generate between 75 and 135 percent more jobs than spending on fossil fuels. With Germany, South Korea and Spain, again, we do not need to match the job increases per $1 million in clean energy investments against job losses through withdrawing $1 million from fossil fuel spending.

Focusing now on the fossil fuel producing countries, why is it that in all six cases, clean energy infrastructures generate more—often significantly more—jobs per $1 million in spending than the existing fossil fuel infrastructure? The reason has nothing to do with climate stabilization per se. There are two separate factors at play.

The first is the higher level of *labor intensity* that results from spending on clean energy. More money is spent on hiring people and less on machines, supplies, and energy consumption. This is not surprising if we imagine channeling investment funds to, for example, hiring construction workers to retrofit buildings or install solar panels as opposed to drilling for oil. We would see a lot more people on the retrofitting job site than at the oil drilling rig relative to the size of the project. The second factor is the *domestic content* of spending—how much money stays within the domestic economy as opposed to buying imports. When an economy retrofits its existing building stock, improves its public transportation system, or invests to install solar panels, a much higher share of overall spending and job creation will remain within the country than when it is purchasing imported oil.

Scaling the Job Effects to 1.5% of GDP

In Table 6.2, showing the employment effects of channeling 1.5 percent of GDP into clean energy investments, we again first see that the differences in the job creation figures between countries are large. Among the fossil fuel producing countries, investing 1.5 percent of GDP on clean energy investments will produce around 250,000 jobs in South Africa, 1.5 million jobs in the U.S., between 925,000 – 950,000 jobs in Brazil and Indonesia, and between 11.4 and 12 million jobs in China and India. For our three fossil fuel importing countries, clean energy investments at 1.5 percent of GDP generates 175,000

Table 6.2 Jobs Generated through Spending 1.5% of GDP
on Clean Energy versus Fossil Fuels

Large-scale Fossil Fuel Producing Countries

	Total Clean Energy Jobs Created through Investing 1.5% of GDP	Net Clean Energy Jobs Created after subtracting Fossil Fuel Job Losses	Clean Energy Job Creation as Share of Total Labor Force	
			Total Job Creation	Net Job Creation
Brazil	925,000	395,000	0.9%	0.4%
China	11.4 million	6.4 million	1.5%	0.6%
India	12.0 million	5.7 million	2.6%	1.4%
Indonesia	954,000	752,000	0.8%	0.6%
South Africa	252,000	126,000	1.4%	0.7%
United States	1.5 million	650,000	1.0%	0.5%

Large-scale Fossil-Fuel Importing Countries

	Total Clean Energy Jobs Created through Investing 1.5% of GDP	Clean Energy Job Creation as Share of Total Labor Force
Germany	330,000	0.8%
Spain	320,000	1.4%
South Korea	175,000	0.6%

Sources: See Pollin et al. (2015a) Chapter 6 and Appendix 2 for estimating methodology.

jobs in South Korea and between 320,000 and 330,000 in Germany and Spain. These large differences are driven both by relative wage rates country-by-country and by large differences in each country's GDP.

But here again, our main interest is with the total levels of jobs *within each country* as well as the net job creation after we subtract jobs lost to the contraction of the fossil fuel industry in our six fossil fuel producing countries. Of course, among the six fossil fuel producing countries, it is not necessarily the case that the country's fossil fuel spending will contract by the same amount that the clean energy economy expands. But this assumption provides a simple illustration of the net job gains that will occur through a clean energy investment project in fossil fuel producing countries—even when the expansion of each country's energy efficiency and renewable energy investments are matched dollar-for-dollar by fossil fuel industry retrenchments.

Table 6.2 also shows, for each country, the level of job creation as a share of each country's overall labor force. These figures are not large, with respect to both the fossil fuel producers as well as the fossil fuel importers. They range between 0.6 and 2.6 percent for total job creation and between 0.4 and 1.4 percent for net job creation, after subtracting the jobs lost through fossil fuel retrenchments—including the cuts in the oil refining sectors in Germany, South Korea and Spain. Of course, we would not expect these job figures to be much larger, given that we are setting the overall increase in clean energy investments (and fossil fuel retrenchments) at no more than 1.5 percent of each country's GDP.

What these figures make clear is that clean energy investment programs, scaled at 1.5 percent of GDP, will not, by themselves, deliver full employment in any given country. But clean energy investments will nevertheless be a positive new source of job opportunities. Certainly these net job increases—roughly 6.4 million in China, 5.7 million in India,

750,000 in Indonesia, 650,000 in the United States, 400,000 in Brazil, 300,000 in Germany and Spain, 175,000 in South Korea, 125,000 in South Africa—are not trivial. Politicians in all nine countries would be very pleased to claim credit for job gains of this magnitude. Moreover, for all countries, clean energy investments will mean more overall job opportunities relative to maintaining the country's existing fossil fuel energy infrastructure. In other words, overall, building clean energy economies in all regions of the world will not require sacrifices by working people. Working people will rather benefit, in many cases substantially, from the overall growth in job opportunities.

At the same time, employment conditions will not improve for *all* workers under all circumstances through clean energy investments. Who is likely to fare better or worse through a clean energy investment agenda? To answer this question, we need to address three additional important issues beyond the figures we present in Tables 6.1 and 6.2: the impact of labor productivity growth over time on job creation, the *quality* of the jobs being generated, and the inevitable difficulties that will be faced by workers dependent on the fossil fuel industry. We take these up in turn.

Labor Productivity Growth and Job Creation

The employment effects reported in Tables 6.1 and 6.2 are based on the production methods currently used in each country. So spending $1 million on clean energy investments will generate, on average, 8.7 million jobs in the United States and 261.9 jobs in India, based on what we know about the current production methods being used today. But clean energy technologies will certainly improve over the twenty-year investment cycle. Such technological improvements will typically increase average labor productivity. This means that fewer workers will be needed to raise energy efficiency levels or expand clean renewable energy production. What will be the impact of such labor productivity improvements on our overall finding that clean energy investments will be a positive source of job creation throughout the world?

In fact, gains in employment opportunities should increase over time, even after we allow that average labor productivity improves every year. Considering past patterns of productivity growth, my co-workers and I find that, since the mid-1990s, the rate at which productivity has improved in the clean energy sectors varies considerably by country. For example, productivity gains have been relatively modest in Brazil, Indonesia, South Africa, and the United States but have been rapid in India and South Korea. Of course, we cannot know from these past productivity trends what is likely to happen moving forward. Still, if anything, we should generally expect labor productivity in the clean energy sectors to accelerate, as a result of much faster rates of investment in these sectors. This should, in turn, encourage innovation and productivity improvements.

Nevertheless, regardless of how slowly or quickly labor productivity improves in various countries, the key to achieving strong gains in employment opportunities is rapid expansion of investment in energy efficiency and clean renewables. Indeed, based again on past economic trends in all countries, it is almost certain that the growth in investment spending and operational activities will outpace improvements in labor productivity. As a result, the expansion in employment opportunities should increase over time, even in countries where labor productivity grows at relatively rapid rates.

Job Quality and Skill Requirements

Increased employment opportunities will be spread widely in all countries. Moreover, the majority of jobs created by clean energy investments will be in the same areas of employment in which people already work. For example, constructing wind farms creates jobs for sheet metal workers, machinists, and truck drivers, among others. Increasing the energy efficiency of buildings through retrofitting relies, among others, on roofers, insulators, and building inspectors. Expanding public transportation systems employs civil engineers, electricians, and dispatchers. Increasing demand for bioenergy will mean a significant increase in employment in standard agricultural activities. At the same time, we do still need to address several issues: where the new employment opportunities are most likely to open up, the likely pay levels and other conditions on these jobs, the likely gender balance among them, and the kinds of new educational and skill requirements that might be needed.

Expanding job opportunities by sector. Three economic sectors, broadly defined, will see relatively large increases in employment. The first is agriculture, where increasing job opportunities will result from the expansion of bioenergy production. Second, construction jobs will also increase substantially, due to both energy efficiency building retrofits and infrastructure investments to upgrade electrical grid and public transportation systems. Third, manufacturing jobs will increase to meet the increased demand for solar panels, wind turbines, and other renewable energy equipment.

Of course, not all countries will expand employment equally in all of these areas. The agriculture and construction jobs will most likely grow in all countries in rough proportion to the overall expansion in clean energy investments, since agriculture and construction activities typically rely mainly on their own domestic work force and other resources. By contrast, many countries will rely on imports to meet at least some of the increased demand for renewable energy manufacturing products. As such, the employment gains through expanding clean energy will be lower when a country purchases imports as opposed to producing these goods domestically. But even when, for example, a country is importing solar panels, a growing reliance on solar energy will still generate more jobs for workers who are transporting, installing, and maintaining the solar equipment as well as upgrading the electrical grid system for transmitting solar power.

Countries importing a large share of their manufactured clean energy products can also consider policies to expand domestic production. When domestic production increases, domestic job opportunities will expand as well. I consider this issue further in Chapter 7, on policy options.

Informal employment. In all but the most advanced economies, employment in agriculture and construction is, at present, mostly informal. This means that there is a high proportion of very small enterprises and self-employment. Most of the time, working in informal enterprises means low pay and benefits and little to no job security.

At the same time, the new agricultural and construction jobs are not necessarily consigned to being bad jobs. The major increase in investment flowing into construction and agriculture could create new opportunities to raise labor standards in these sectors. For example, in Brazil, the expansion of its bioenergy sectors has slowly encouraged increased agricultural mechanization and rising productivity. The growth of employment resulting from Brazil's bioenergy investments has therefore been less than it would have been if traditional agriculture methods had continued to prevail and productivity had consequently remained low. But this mechanization trend does also create greater opportunities for better pay and working conditions for the large numbers of jobs that will remain in agriculture. Of course, nobody should expect that mechanization and faster productivity growth will, by themselves, deliver better jobs. But such gains in productivity will create new opportunities for workers and their representatives, along with public policymakers, to support major upgrades in labor standards.

Opportunities for women. Throughout the world, the construction and manufacturing sectors are heavily dominated by male workers. If this situation were to continue, clean energy investments that rely heavily on construction and manufacturing would yield relatively few new employment opportunities for women. These investment areas include hydro, wind, solar, and geothermal power, as well as efficiency investments in building retrofits and electrical grid upgrades. The share of female employment generated by these clean energy investment areas ranges between 20 and 30 percent in most countries, including both advanced and developing economies. Clean energy investment projects should be used as an opportunity to highlight the need for much greater gender equity in these currently male-dominated areas.

Education and skill requirements. The general level of educational attainment for workers in the clean energy sectors is not, for the most part, significantly different than those for workers presently employed in the oil, coal, and natural gas sectors. Thus, as jobs in the fossil fuel sectors are reduced, there will be an increased supply of workers available to operate within the clean energy sectors with appropriate levels of general educational credentials.

At the same time, some of the newly created jobs generated by clean energy investments will also require new skills. For example, installing solar panels on roofs and wiring these panels so they supply electricity are distinct tasks relative to the jobs that are traditionally performed by either roofers or electricians. Similarly, refining agricultural wastes into biofuels is different than refining corn into ethanol or, for that matter, refining petroleum into gasoline. Countries advancing clean energy investment projects will need to make provisions for these and similar areas that demand new types of training and skill acquisition. But how extensive will be the need for new training and skills?

A recent study by the International Labour Office, *Skills for Green Jobs: A Global View*, concluded that clean energy and other green-economy occupations will, for the most part, require updating existing skills as opposed to training workers for entirely new occupations. For example, the authors observe that:

> The number of existing occupations that will change and update their skills content by far exceeds the number of new occupations that will emerge.... The greening of established occupations implies incremental changes in qualifications. New skills are needed because specific competencies are currently lacking [and] some existing skills relating to job tasks that become obsolete cease to be used.[3]

Inevitably, there will be some difficult transition periods and bottlenecks in most countries as the growth in clean energy investments generates increasing demands for workers with new types of specific skills. Still, these bottlenecks will be less severe than they might be otherwise. This is because, as we have discussed, most jobs and skill requirements in the clean energy economy are not significantly different than those already required of most people currently working in other sectors. In addition, the general educational attainment levels for most jobs within the clean energy sectors will be roughly comparable to those within the fossil fuel sectors facing retrenchments. The net result is an increase in the number of workers that can move into clean energy. In addition, countries facing shortages of skilled workers in specific areas can rely on imports to cover these gaps until the country's own supply of qualified workers expands.

Just Transition for Fossil Fuel Sector Workers

There is no denying that workers and communities throughout the world whose livelihoods depend on people consuming oil, coal, and natural gas will lose out in the clean energy transition. In order for the global clean energy project to succeed, it must provide adequate transitional support for these workers and communities.

The United Nations Environmental Program (UNEP) addressed this issue in a 2008 study, *Green Jobs: Toward Decent Work in a Sustainable, Low-Carbon World*. The authors describe what they term a "fair and just transition" for workers and communities that are currently dependent on the fossil fuel industries:

> The shift to a low carbon and sustainable society must be as equitable as possible. . . . From the point of view of social solidarity, and in order to mobilize the political and workplace-based support for the changes that are needed, it is imperative that policies be put in place to ensure that those who

> are likely to be negatively affected are protected
> through income support, retraining opportunities,
> relocation assistance and the like.[4]

The arguments made in this study for a "fair and just transition" build from the ideas of late U.S. labor and environmental leader Tony Mazzocchi, who developed the idea of a "Superfund" for workers who lose their jobs as a result of necessary environmental transitions. Mazzocchi's use of the term refers to the U.S. environmental program that was implemented in 1980 to clean up sites at which corporations had dumped hazardous wastes from petrochemical, oil, and nuclear energy production. As Mazzocchi wrote as early as 1993:

> Paying people to make the transition from one kind
> of economy—from one kind of job—to another is
> not welfare. Those who work with toxic materials on a daily basis...in order to provide the world
> with the energy and the materials it needs deserve a
> helping hand to make a new start in life. . . . There
> is a Superfund for dirt. There ought to be one for
> workers.[5]

The critical point in Mazzocchi's idea is that providing high-quality adjustment assistance to today's fossil fuel industry workers will represent a major contribution toward making a global climate stabilization project viable. It is a matter of simple justice, but it is also a matter of strategic politics. Without such adjustment assistance programs operating at a major scale, the workers and communities facing retrenchment from the clean energy investment project will, predictably and understandably, fight to defend their communities and livelihoods. This in turn will create unacceptable delays in proceeding with effective climate stabilization policies.

Still, the impact on workers and communities from retrenchments in the fossil fuel sectors will not depend only on the level of support provided through explicit adjustment assistance programs, no matter how generous their provisions. The broader set of economic opportunities available to workers will also be critical. The fact that the clean energy investment project will itself generate a net expansion in employment in all regions of the globe means that there will be new opportunities for displaced fossil fuel sector workers within the energy industry itself. There will be more jobs for, among other occupations, operations managers, mechanical engineers, construction managers, farmers and ranchers, roofers, electricians, and sheet metal workers.

But further than this, the single best form of protection for displaced workers in all countries is an economy that operates at full employment. A full employment economy is simply one in which there is an abundance of decent jobs available for all people seeking work. In a full employment economy, the challenges faced by displaced workers—regardless of the reasons for their having become displaced—are greatly diminished simply because they should be able to find another decent job without excessive difficulties. It also follows that, in a full employment economy, the costs to taxpayers of providing reasonable levels of financial support for displaced workers would be greatly diminished. Overall then, in the realm of overarching social, economic, and environmental policy priorities, a commitment to full employment should be understood as fully consistent with and supportive of the project of building a clean energy economy.

Reducing annual global CO_2 emissions by 40 percent within twenty years—from its current level of 33 billion tons to 20 billion tons, from 4.6 to 2.3 tons per capita—is a realistic goal. What we need to do is straightforward: first, increase global investments ever year in energy efficiency and clean renewables by 1.5 percent of global GDP, and second, over this twenty-year period, cut oil, coal, and natural gas consumption by 33 percent, amounting to an average reduction of 2.3 percent per year. If these two projects are implemented, global per capita CO_2 emissions will fall by 40 percent within twenty years.

But whether something like this scenario will actually happen is another matter. Converting it from a plan to a reality will require governments around the world to implement effective policies, and this, in turn will require political will. Our topic in this chapter is what will constitute effective policies. We save political will for Chapter 8.

I am not in a position to instruct policymakers on what exactly should be done in any particular country to advance a viable clean energy project. My goal here is much more modest: to present a sketch of a policy framework that should have broad applicability for countries within all regions of the globe, at all levels of development. I focus on three areas. First: designing industrial policies that can successfully navigate the challenges of technological development and adaptation, as well as mobilize adequate amounts of affordable financing to pay for clean energy investments at the required scale. Second: understanding the opportunities that should emerge for alternative ownership forms in the energy industry other than the private corporations and giant state enterprises that dominate at present. And third: examining the implications of a clean energy transformation on the imports and export accounts of any given country, those relatively rich or poor in their endowments of oil, coal, and natural gas.

Industrial Policies to Build Clean Energy Economies

In all countries throughout the world, effective industrial policies will be necessary to achieve a successful clean energy transformation. Depending on specific conditions within each country, industrial policies will be needed to promote technical innovations and, even more broadly, adaptations of existing clean energy technologies. Again depending on circumstances, governments will need to deploy a combination of industrial policy instruments, including research and development support, preferential tax treatment for clean energy investments, preferential financing arrangements, and government purchasing policies. Clean energy industrial policies will also need to include regulations of both fossil fuel and clean energy prices as well as emission standards. We now consider some of the key policy questions at stake.

Can Industrial Policies Work?

This needs to be the first question we consider, especially given that, from a free market perspective, the answer is almost invariably a resounding "no." According to that point of view, governments should not be in the business of subsidizing a particular technology, industry, or location, much less a business firm. This amounts to governments picking winners, which they are incapable of accomplishing effectively. On top of this, industrial policies of this sort force taxpayers to finance the inept efforts at picking winners. In fact, the job of picking winners in the economy is accomplished successfully only when private businesses compete in a free market to satisfy the demands of consumers. Some businesses' decisions will be good, and others will be bad. But what constitutes good versus bad decisions will be sorted out through competitive markets, at no expense to taxpayers.

However, this free market perspective does not accord with the actual trajectories of virtually all countries, in all historical epochs, which have experienced successful industrial development. One critical case in point is technological development in the United States. As Vernon Ruttan made clear in his 2006 book *Is War Necessary for Economic Growth?*, nearly all major technical innovations within the U.S. economy—including, just since the 1940s, jet aviation, computers, nuclear power, and the internet—have entailed huge expenses over long gestation periods. Such expenses could only be managed by the federal government, the Pentagon in particular. Ruttan summarized the matter as follows:

> Can the private sector be relied on as a source of major new general purpose technologies?

The quick response is that it *cannot*. When new technologies are radically different from existing technologies and the gains from advances in technology are so diffuse that they are difficult to capture by the firm conducting the research, private firms have only weak incentives to invest in scientific research or technology development.[1]

Of course, we do not expect that all countries will need or want to attempt to advance the technological frontier with clean energy projects. But all countries will need to successfully *adapt and integrate* clean energy technologies into their economies. This role for industrial policies is described well in Mariana Mazzucato's 2014 book *The Entrepreneurial State*, in which she argues:

> Governments have a leading role to play in supporting the development of clean technologies past their prototypical states through to their commercial viability. Reaching technological 'maturing' requires more support directed to prepare, organize, and stabilize a healthy 'market,' where investment is reasonably low risk and profits can be made.[2]

Creating Large and Stable Clean Energy Markets

A major policy intervention that can facilitate the creation of a vibrant domestic market for clean energy will be for governments to themselves become both large-scale investors in energy efficiency and purchasers of clean renewable energy. In the process of bringing the internet to commercial scale, the U.S. military provided a guaranteed market for thirty-five years, which

enabled the technology to incubate while private investors grad-
ually developed effective commercialization strategies. In fact,
the U.S. military is playing a somewhat comparable role at present with respect to clean energy technologies. It has committed that fully 25 percent of all of its energy purchases will come
from renewable sources by 2025. To the extent that all government agencies, in the United States and elsewhere, make similar
commitments, this will lead to major expansions in clean energy
production, which in turn will accelerate technical innovations
and increase opportunities in the private energy markets.

We have already discussed in Chapter 3 the importance of
setting a price on carbon emissions, through either a carbon
tax or carbon cap. Such measures will raise the market prices
of oil, coal, and natural gas to reflect the enormous costs and
risks imposed on societies by ongoing CO_2 emissions. Raising
the prices for fossil fuels will also, of course, create increased
incentives for both energy efficiency and clean renewable
investments.

But guaranteeing a market with stable prices for clean renewables is also critical here. Such policies fall under so-called *feed-
in tariffs*. These are contracts that require utility companies to
purchase electricity from private renewable energy generators
at prices fixed by long-term contracts. Feed-in tariffs were first
implemented in the United States in the 1970s, and a number of state and local programs are currently operational in
the United States today. However, the impact of feed-in tariffs
have been much more significant outside of the United States,
especially in Germany, Spain, and Canada. A 2009 study by the
U.S. Department of Energy found that these policies in Europe
have "resulted in quick and substantial renewable energy
capacity expansion."[3] The key factor in the success of these

European programs is straightforward: the guaranteed prices for renewable energy have been set to adequately reflect the costs of producing the energy along with a profit for the energy provider. This then encourages private renewable energy investors by providing a stable long-term market environment.

Providing Cheap and Accessible Financing

Financing policies will play a major role in supporting large-scale clean energy investments in all country settings. The case of Germany is instructive, since it has been the most successful large advanced economy to date in developing its clean energy economy. The German government's financing policies have been critical, for example, to its success in implementing high efficiency standards. The overview of the International Energy Agency's 2013 *Energy Efficiency Market Report* focuses precisely on this point, as follows:

> Germany is a world leader in energy efficiency. Germanys' state-owned development bank, KfW, plays a crucial role by providing loans and subsidies for investment in energy efficiency measures in buildings and industry, which have leveraged significant private funds.[4]

Clean energy financing policies have been equally important for developing countries and need to become even more so moving forward. The 2008 World Bank study *Financing Energy Efficiency: Lessons from Brazil, China, India and Beyond* describes 10 case studies of alternative energy efficiency financing structures that are achieving positive results.[5] These include a loan guarantee program for private energy efficiency financing in China, which began in 2003, the development of the Indian

Renewable Energy Development Agency to provide subsidized loans for both renewable and energy efficiency investments, and Brazil's public benefit "wire-charge" mechanism, through which 1 percent of annual utility net revenues are utilized for renewable and energy efficiency investments.

Stephen Spratt, Stephanie Griffith-Jones, and Jose Antonio Ocampo emphasize a further major issue with respect to financing clean energy projects in low-income countries in their 2013 study *Mobilizing Investment for Inclusive Green Growth in Low-Income Countries*— that the benefits of clean energy investments be shared at least equally by the society's least advantaged groups. This would include expanding access to electricity, and providing clean energy for electricity and other needs at affordable prices. To accomplish this, they emphasize that it is not realistic to expect clean energy investments to consistently generate big profits for private businesses:

> Achieving growth that is both green and inclusive is inherently difficult. Doing so using private investment which requires very high returns may be impossible. Unless investors can be persuaded to adopt more reasonable expectations, alternative sources of finance may be needed if the goal of generating inclusive green growth in low-income countries is to be achieved.[6]

The requirement that the financing terms for clean energy investments be affordable for borrowers—that is, not always yielding high returns for lenders—suggests a major role for public investment banks to play. For example, the recently established New Development Bank (NDB), whose founding member countries include Brazil, China, India, Russia, and South Africa, could become a leader in developing innovative and affordable financing arrangements for clean energy investments throughout the developing world. National development banks could play a similar role, as they have traditionally in advancing manufacturing industries within their own countries. As Alice Amsden concluded in *The Rise of 'The Rest'*, her classic work on the development of manufacturing industries in developing countries, "From the viewpoint of long-term capital supply for *public and private investment*, development banks throughout 'the rest' were of overwhelming importance."[7]

Prospects for Alternative Ownership Forms

Beyond the need for development banking, the difficulty of meeting the high profit requirements of large private corporations raises the question: How might alternative ownership forms—including public ownership, community ownership, and small-scale private companies—play a major role in advancing the clean energy investment agenda?

In fact, throughout the world, the energy sector has long operated under a variety of ownership structures, including public/municipal ownership, and various forms of private cooperative ownership in addition to private corporate entities. The alternative ownership forms operate in all areas of the energy industry, including both the fossil fuel and renewable sectors.

Indeed, in the oil and natural gas industry, publicly owned national companies control approximately 90 percent of the world's reserves and 75 percent of production. They also control many of the oil and gas infrastructure systems. These national corporations include Saudi Aramco, Gazprom in Russia, China National Petroleum Corporation, the National

Iranian Oil Company, Petroleos de Venezuela, Petrobras in Brazil, and Petronas in Malaysia. None of these publicly owned companies operates with the same profit imperatives as big private energy corporations such as ExxonMobil, British Petroleum, and Royal Dutch Shell. But this does not mean that they are prepared to commit to fighting climate change simply because we face a global environmental emergency. Just as with the private companies, producing and selling fossil fuel energy generates huge revenue flows for these companies. National development projects, lucrative careers, and political power all depend on continuing the flow of large fossil fuel revenues. We should therefore not expect that public ownership of energy companies will, by itself, provide a more favorable framework for advancing effective clean energy industrial policies.

At the same time, the development of clean energy systems does open opportunities for smaller-scale enterprises, which could be organized through various combinations of public, private and cooperative ownership structures. The European industry, in particular, operates with a high proportion of cooperative ownership forms. The performance of these non-corporate business enterprises has generally been quite favorable relative to the traditional corporate firms. One area where this has been clear is community-based wind farms in Western Europe, especially Germany, Denmark, Sweden, and the United Kingdom.

Mark Bolinger at the U.S. Department of Energy, along with other researchers, has highlighted four important advantages to community ownership structures in the wind industry over traditional corporate ownership.[8] These include:

- *Acceptance of lower rates of profit.* Community-based wind projects in Europe have been able to rely on a wide array of relatively small-scale local investors, whose profit requirements are lower than those of private corporations. This in turn means that the costs of expanding wind power capacity falls, promoting a more rapid expansion in new investments.

- *Increased public support.* Direct community ownership of wind projects has raised public awareness in Europe and increased the number of local people who have direct financial stakes in such projects. This has reduced community resistance to projects at the planning and permitting stages.

- *Potential for lower electricity transmission costs.* The relatively small size of community-owned projects enables them to be more easily located within, or nearby, the communities themselves. This makes possible significant reductions in the costs of transmitting energy over the grid. Such benefits can be especially large when community wind projects are established in more densely populated areas. For example, in Copenhagen as of 2005, two community-owned wind projects were operating within the city limits.

- *Electricity price stability.* Community-owned wind projects operate at arms-length from the two forces that are most responsible for creating instability in electricity prices: the global market for oil and the speculative commodities futures market for energy, including electricity. Because, by their basic ownership structure, community-based wind projects will continue to operate independently of the global price of oil as well as the commodities futures markets, this should create long-term conditions supportive of electricity price stability.

Of course, community-based wind projects also come with disadvantages. The most significant is that community-owned projects will tend to be smaller in scale than corporate-owned wind farms. Large-scale corporate wind farms are thus better equipped to spread the costs of any given project, including permitting and legal costs and the full range of construction and transmission costs. However, the experiences in Germany, Denmark, Sweden, and the United Kingdom make clear that community-based ownership structures can succeed in the wind industry. It is also true that the incentive structure and regulatory environment in Europe are more supportive of community-based models. The most important factor here is the prevalence of feed-in tariffs in Europe. As discussed above, these feed-in laws guarantee fixed long-term prices and access to the grid for small-scale producers.

The development of affordable renewable energy is also, increasingly, creating realistic prospects for private individuals, businesses, and small-scale community organizations to own their own renewable energy supplies that are off the grid altogether. These *distributed energy* supply systems are powered by solar, wind, and other renewable sources. In January 2015, the *Financial Times* reported that "across the U.S., about 45,300 businesses and 596,000 homes have solar panels. . . . Over the past four years, the numbers have risen threefold for businesses and fourfold for homes, as the costs of solar power have plunged."[9] This trend has led the Edison Electric Institute, the U.S. electricity utility industry association, to warn that that the utilities were facing "disruptive challenges" comparable to the way that the traditional landline telephone industry was shaken up by the emergence of mobile telephone technology. As this development proceeds, it will continue to create expanding opportunities for alternative small-scale ownership forms within the emerging clean energy economy.

100% Community-Owned Renewable Supply in Rural Germany

The viability of small-scale community-owned clean energy systems is underscored by the recent experiences in Freiamt, a rural community of 4,200 residents in Germany's Black Forest region. As of 2008, Freiamt had achieved 100 percent electric power supply through community-owned renewable sources. Wind energy is Freiamt's main power source, but they also generate smaller amounts of energy from solar PV, biogas, and small-scale hydro plants.

One of the most compelling aspects of the Freiamt experience has been that individual and community interests, not environmental concerns, were the primary motives for developing the 100 percent renewable energy model. Indeed, after having surveyed the residents of Freiamt, a research team led by Liwan Li of the University of California, Berkeley, emphasized that the project would not have succeeded on the basis of the residents' environmental goals alone, even though such environmental concerns were foremost for policymaking bodies outside the community. Li and his coauthors summarize the sources of the success of the project as follows:

> The residents' motivations for undertaking the project were strongly connected to community-interest as opposed to awareness of climate change which is generally far more distantly connected with their daily life. The residents and local government were more concerned about their own benefit

from the project and its influences on their local
surroundings. They create new income streams,
have positive effects on the community's image
and are a way to strengthen rural areas by establishing a regional value added chain. . . . Especially for
rural areas, energy projects are a chance to foster
regional development, to secure agricultural holdings and to conserve cultural landscapes that have
been shaped by agriculture over centuries.[10]

The case of Freiamt demonstrates the major opportunities
of advancing clean energy alternatives in a wide range of settings, assuming a supportive policy environment. Freiamt is not
endowed with large supplies of wind, sun, geothermal or hydro
power. It is also not especially affluent or associated with any
kind of high-technology business enterprises or research centers.
The Freiamt experience also demonstrates that the benefits of
small-scale renewable power systems extend beyond climate stabilization. Freiamt shows that the clean energy transformation
can become a foundation for strengthening rural communities
in ways that also yield immediate tangible gains for community
members.

Imports, Exports, and the "Resource Curse"[11]

A major factor that will enable the large-scale growth of a country's clean energy industries over the next twenty years is that
the fossil fuel industries will contract at the same time. We have
already discussed how this pattern will generate an overall rise in
job opportunities, since the growth of job opportunities through
clean energy investments will exceed the loss of jobs through
retrenchments in oil, coal, and natural gas. But this pattern will

also affect economies more broadly. Across the board, there will be far less demand for businesses that extract, transport, refine, and distribute fossil fuels—down to the retail service stations where people buy gasoline and the trucking companies that deliver propane gas to homeowners. The businesses that sell supplies to support these activities will also see their markets decline sharply over time.

These large-scale shifts between the clean energy and fossil fuel sectors will take place in all countries, regardless of whether a country relies mainly on its own domestic resources for its fossil fuel supplies. Consider the cases of the three major economies that we discussed in Chapter 6 that are heavy fossil fuel importers. As of 2012, Germany imported 60 percent of the energy it consumes, and fossil fuels accounted for 78 percent of its total energy consumption. South Korea imported 82 percent of its total energy supply, and fossil fuels accounted for 83 percent of its total energy consumption. Spain imported 75 percent of its total energy consumption, and fossil fuels accounted for 80 percent of total consumption.

Overall, these three countries will benefit greatly through reducing their dependency on imported energy. As we saw in Chapter 6, jobs will expand to a proportionally greater extent than in countries in which the rise of the clean energy sectors is matched by a decline in their domestic fossil fuel production. In addition, the fact that these countries will spend less on imports will free up a large new source of domestic funding to help finance the country's clean energy investment projects.[12] At the same time, the domestic industries in these countries engaged in refining, transporting, and marketing oil will contract. Jobs will be lost and businesses will shut down. As we discussed in Chapter 6, government policies will need to focus on supporting workers and communities through these transitions. A major resource for supporting successful transitions will be the expansion in opportunities that will occur in each country's clean energy sectors.

Countries that export fossil fuels will face greater challenges, starting with the loss of their export revenues. However, many countries have already successfully navigated similar transitions. For example, Indonesia had long been a major exporter of both oil and coal before its oil exports began to fall substantially in the 1990s. In 2003, Indonesia began importing more oil than it exports, and in 2009, it suspended its membership in OPEC—the Oil Producing Exporting Countries. Indonesia did still continue to be a large-scale exporter of coal. Nevertheless, its overall fossil fuel export revenues—including sales of both oil and coal exports—fell by 35 percent as a share of GDP between 2001 and 2010. Despite this, Indonesia's overall GDP still grew at generally healthy rates.

All else equal, the Indonesian economy would almost certainly benefit from exporting larger amounts of both oil and coal. But the fact that the decline in Indonesia's fossil fuel exports did not correspond with a similar decline in its overall GDP growth means that the country has demonstrated its capacity to adjust to the fall in its oil exports. Transitioning into a clean energy investment project will require still further adaptations, since this will mean further cuts in oil exports along with major declines in coal exports. But Indonesia's experience since the decline in its oil export revenues suggests that it can manage this transition successfully.

Indonesia's experience also raises an important broader question. Do countries endowed with large-scale fossil fuel resources necessarily end up better off than resource-poor countries?

Indeed, there is a long-standing debate among economists as to whether countries with rich endowments of fossil fuel resources are "cursed." The idea is that various groups within an oil-rich country will devote excessive amounts of time and effort to fighting over who can grab the biggest bounty from these oil revenues, as opposed to focusing on developing well-functioning economies. This pattern helps to explain why the nine countries in Sub-Saharan Africa that have been oil exporters for several years—Angola, Cameroon, Chad, the Republic of Congo, Ivory Coast, Equatorial Guinea, Gabon, and Nigeria—have not, in general, performed better than the rest of the continent in expanding economic well-being and reducing poverty. Of course, countries are not necessarily cursed by having major oil reserves. In all cases, a wide range of factors will determine whether large-scale oil revenues can deliver broadly shared benefits.

By the same token, in all regions throughout the global economy, the key to a successful clean energy transition is not relying on major fossil fuel energy resources today but advancing effective policies that will deliver high levels of energy efficiency, affordable clean renewable energy supplies, an abundance of new job opportunities, and a just transition for fossil fuel workers and communities facing retrenchments.

"De-growth" as a Solution?

As an alternative to the set of policies we have reviewed, is there a case to be made for requiring countries—all countries, or perhaps only the rich and middle-income countries—to forego economic growth as a necessary means for reducing their emissions levels? In recent years, a large number of progressive economists and others have advanced such anti-growth or "de-growth" perspectives.[13] According to this view, economic growth is fundamentally incompatible with climate stabilization and ecological sustainability more generally. In addition, according to this perspective, economic growth is also responsible for rising inequality, as income gains from growth flow ever-more disproportionately to the rich. De-growth proponents further argue that people in growing economies rely excessively on obtaining ever-more consumer goods as the means to achieve happiness. Meanwhile, the expansion in the supply of consumer goods is taken to be the primary driver of the need for economic growth—and the consumption of fossil fuel energy to power this growth.

But this perspective is far too sweeping in its indictment of economic growth. Consider some simple arithmetic. We know that global CO_2 emissions need to fall from its current level of 33 billion tons to 20 billion tons within twenty years. As we have seen, after accounting for population growth, this amounts to an emissions cut from 4.6 to 2.3 tons per capita. Under a de-growth scenario, assume that global GDP contracts by 10 percent over the next two decades. That would entail a reduction of global GDP four times larger than what we experienced over the 2007–09 financial crisis and Great Recession. In terms of CO_2 emissions, the net effect of this 10 percent GDP contraction, considered on its own, would be to push emissions down by precisely 10 percent—that is, from 33 to 30 billion tons. So the global economy would still not even come close to hitting the 2035 emissions reduction target of 20 billion tons.

What this example makes clear is that, even under a de-growth scenario, the main force that will drive emissions levels down is *not* a contraction of overall GDP but huge *expansions* in energy efficiency and clean renewable energy investments and correspondingly massive cuts in the use of fossil fuel energy sources. Within the framework of a transformative global clean energy project—with clean energy investments expanding rapidly as fossil fuels contract—any reductions in overall economic growth will be only a minor sideshow as a source of emissions reductions.

Moreover, global growth contraction would result in massive job losses and declines in living standards. Global unemployment rose by over 30 million during the Great Recession. I have not seen in any of the de-growth literature a reasonable argument as to how a huge contraction in global GDP wouldn't generate a comparable loss of global job opportunities. It is true that, for nearly forty years now, the gains from economic growth in virtually all countries have persistently favored the rich. Yet it is also true that the prospects for reversing inequality in all countries will be far greater when the overall economy is growing than when the rich are fighting everyone else for shares of a shrinking pie.

In short, a de-growth approach to climate stabilization is incapable, on its own, of delivering significant cuts in CO_2 emissions. It is also untenable on ethical grounds because of the impact it would have on the economic prospects for working people and the poor. But even thinking strictly in strategic terms alone, attempting to implement a de-growth agenda would have the effect of rendering the global clean energy project as utterly unrealistic politically.

This is exactly the opposite of what we need now, which is a global clean energy project that is truly capable of raising mass living standards in all regions of the world while also driving global CO_2 emissions down to 20 billion tons by 2035.

8 Risk, Ethics, and the Politics of Climate Stabilization

The clean energy investment program I have outlined demonstrates that a viable global program for climate stabilization is within reach. The key is to recognize that the prospects for dramatically expanding investments in energy efficiency and clean renewable energy are highly favorable. We can support this conclusion through reviewing evidence from around the globe as to the costs, on average, of achieving 1 Q-BTU of energy efficiency or expanding the supply of solar, wind, geothermal, small-scale hydro or low-emissions bioenergy by 1 Q-BTU. Equally critically, we have seen that advancing the clean energy investment project will not be derailed by high-cost trade-offs—between job opportunities, economic growth, and an adequate energy supply on the one hand and the environment, a stable climate, and public safety, on the other.

But a global clean energy transformation will never succeed on the basis of cost calculations alone. As discussed in Chapter 7, we also need policy frameworks in all regions of the globe that are well designed and effectively implemented. These will include measures not only to dramatically expand clean energy investments but also to dramatically cut the consumption of oil, coal, and natural gas while protecting the workers and communities whose livelihoods currently depend on the fossil fuel industries.

Yet even with the evidence on costs and benefits and a viable policy framework all pushing in the right direction, there is still no guarantee the clean energy transformation will succeed. We also need to confront a broader set of fundamental issues at play. These issues move us beyond questions of costs, trade-offs, and policy design, and into matters of risk assessment, ethics, and politics.

Clean Energy Investments as Climate Change Insurance

The overwhelming consensus among qualified scientists is that global climate change is real. This consensus view is also clear that the single most important cause of climate change is CO_2 emissions generated by burning oil, coal, and natural gas to produce energy. The consensus position is well represented through the research and publications supported by the IPCC.

The consensus is also clear that the harm likely to be caused by climate change is enormous. We began Chapter 1 with observations by Prof. Kerry Emanuel of MIT. As we saw, Emanuel warns that, over the coming decades, the effects of unchecked climate change could include intense heat waves, previously fertile areas becoming barren, the spread of blights on natural vegetation and crops, and massive flooding in coastal regions throughout the world. Emmanuel believes these disasters could in turn lead to famines, the spread of disease and mass migrations. Many climate scientists argue further that climate change poses an existential threat to a large number of plant and animal species.

We must keep these warnings in focus. But we must also recognize that not all scientists accept this consensus position. For decades, a small minority of researchers has questioned the consensus view on several grounds. Their perspectives include the following: climate change is occurring, but its causes are unknown; the primary causes of climate change are natural, not human, processes; climate change is occurring, but it is unlikely to produce serious negative consequences; and the IPCC's estimates as to how quickly emissions need to fall to stabilize the climate are not reliable.

Some researchers advancing skeptical views have been funded by right-wing think tanks and the fossil fuel industry. But how important is this consideration in itself? In fact, many researchers on the other side of the argument receive financial support from environmental organizations (as do some economists, including myself). In any case, no matter where the funding comes from, the findings of the researcher still have to stand or fall on their merits.

This is especially true since we know that the history of science and technology abounds with examples in which mainstream consensus positions were later overturned. In the 1950s, the consensus position among nuclear physicists and engineers was that nuclear power would rapidly become a low-cost and reliable source of electricity. Sixty years later, the average costs of nuclear electricity generation are higher than those for fossil fuels, wind, geothermal, or bioenergy. Considering my own field of economics just prior to the 2007–09 global financial crisis and Great Recession, the mainstream consensus position was that financial markets were self-regulating and operated most effectively without government interference. Most mainstream

economists at that time regarded government regulations to promote financial stability as vestiges of outmoded thinking.

In short, it is fully within the spirit of honest scientific inquiry
to allow for the possibility, however small, that the consensus
perspective on climate change, as represented by the IPCC and
other research bodies, is wrong. But this possibility does then
raise an extremely important question: Could we end up wasting
trillions of dollars, and disrupting hundreds of fossil-fuel dependent communities, to build a global clean energy economy
when, in the end, such efforts would have been unnecessary?

In fact, even after we allow for the possibility that the consensus perspective is wrong, the case for taking action now to
stabilize the climate remains overwhelming. We need to take
action now, not on the basis of absolute certainty about the
causes or consequences of climate change, but rather on the
basis of reasonable probabilities. Indeed, we need to think of the
global clean energy project as the equivalent of an insurance policy to protect ourselves and the planet against the serious prospect—though not the certainty—that the types of consequences
described by Kerry Emanuel and others could occur.

We purchase insurance to protect ourselves against many
other contingencies, such as house fires, automobile accidents,
and serious illnesses. We do this even though we have no idea
whether our house may ever burn down or we may experience a serious car accident. From this perspective, the argument in support of a global clean energy project as a climate
change insurance policy is indisputable—even if we allow for
the small possibility that the consensus scientific position on
climate change is wrong. The only serious matter in dispute is
how much we should be willing to pay to purchase an adequate
amount of climate change insurance. This is the equivalent of

deciding not *whether* to purchase automobile insurance but *how much* to spend and how much coverage we need.

Many legitimate considerations and differences will emerge in answering this question. At the same time, the clear conclusion to be drawn on the basis of the analysis in the previous chapters of this book is that the costs of the global clean energy project will be relatively low and will be mostly contained within one sector of the economy—the fossil fuel sector.

It is true that, relative to the International Energy Agency's BAU scenario, I am proposing to spend an additional 1.5 percent of global GDP every year for at least the next twenty years on energy efficiency and clean renewable energy investments. Assuming an average global GDP growth rate of 3.4 percent over this period (as in the IEA's BAU model), the total global spending bill over the twenty-year cycle will amount to roughly \$30 trillion. This is hardly pocket change. However, these expenditures cannot be fairly evaluated through considering the cost side of the ledger alone. Energy efficiency and clean renewable energy investments will also yield substantial net human and ecological benefits even in the short run, as well as establishing an effective level of global climate change insurance in the long run.

As we have seen, energy efficiency investments will be the first driving force pushing global CO_2 emissions down by 40 percent over the next twenty years. But in the short term, energy efficiency investments will also deliver lower costs of energy services for all consumers in all regions of the globe—lower costs to operate buildings, cooking equipment, mobile phones, automobiles, airplanes, trains, and all forms of industrial machinery. Clean renewable energy investments will be the second driver pushing down global CO_2 emissions. To a significant extent at present, and increasingly over the next twenty years as investment expands, clean renewables will be able to deliver energy at costs roughly equal to or lower than those from non-renewable energy sources. This will be even more likely if the environmental costs of burning fossil fuels are incorporated, as they should be, in market prices and fossil fuel subsidies are eliminated. At the same time, expanding clean renewable energy production will create extensive new opportunities for small-scale community-based energy systems. An especially important benefit here is that community-based energy systems can eliminate the need to construct new large-scale utility-based operations in regions of the world where such systems have never been built.

Investments in energy efficiency and clean renewable energy will produce further major benefits, in both the short- and longer terms. As discussed in detail in Chapter 6, these investments will be a significant new engine of job creation, in all regions of the global, for countries at all levels of development. This will be true even after we fully account for the job losses that will inevitably result from the contraction of the global fossil fuel industry. The declines in CO_2 emissions generated by the clean energy investment project will also substantially reduce air pollution. This, in turn, will produce major health benefits, as I discussed briefly in Chapter 1.

Of course, transitioning out of fossil fuels will entail real costs. The workers and communities throughout the world whose livelihoods depend on the fossil fuel industry will inevitably be hurt. But these impacts can be diminished through effective transitional policies. This is precisely why I have emphasized the importance of measures to advance a truly just transition for affected workers and communities. Such measures need to be a central element of the overall clean energy investment project, not a mere appendage to the plan.

After accounting for the full range of factors at play with the global clean energy project, we can conclude, on balance, that the costs of purchasing global climate change insurance will be modest. It is an insurance policy we can unquestionably afford to pay, even if, in the unlikely event, the prevailing scientific consensus on climate change does turn out to be wrong. The alternative to not purchasing this insurance policy is, effectively, to play Russian roulette with the fate of the earth.

Global Fairness

It is one thing to conclude that "we"—meaning all people and countries living on planet earth—should, without question, pay for global climate change insurance, in the form of 1.5 percent of GDP per year in energy efficiency and clean renewable investments. But it is another matter to determine what standard of fairness should be applied in allocating the costs of this insurance policy among the various people, countries, and regions of the globe. It is obviously not fair to suggest that everyone on earth needs to pay for global climate insurance at the same fixed rate. But how should we allocate these costs fairly?

If the clean energy investment project proposed in this book is successful, average per capita CO_2 emissions will fall within twenty years from its current level of 4.6 tons to 2.3 tons. But within the framework I have developed, at the end of the twenty-year project, average U.S. emissions will be 5.8 tons per capita, nearly three times the averages for China and the world as a whole, and five times the average for India. At a basic level, this is of course unfair. It is particularly unfair given that, over the past century of the fossil fuel era, U.S. emissions have exceeded those in India and China combined by around 400 percent.[1]

In the name of fairness, one could, with good reason, insist that the United States and other rich countries be required to bring down per capita CO_2 emissions to the same level as low-income countries. We could also insist that high-income people—regardless of their countries of residence—be permitted to generate no more CO_2 emissions than anyone else. That would include no exceptions for families owning one or more large private residences or for professors traveling great distances to discuss climate change stabilization at international conferences.

There is a solid ethical case for such measures. But there is also absolutely no chance that they will be implemented. What is the point of demanding something that is impossible to achieve? Focus for the moment on the U.S. case. On grounds of both ethics and realism, it seems much more constructive to require that, in addition to bringing its own emissions down to about 6 tons per capita within twenty years, the United States must also assist other countries to finance and bring to scale their own transformative clean energy projects.

The case of Indonesia is illustrative. In 2012, Indonesia's per capita GDP was around $3,500, which places it among the lower middle-income countries. Its per capita carbon emissions were roughly a tenth of those of the United States. But Indonesia aims to growth rapidly over the next twenty years, in the range of 6 to 7 percent annually. The Indonesian government also projects a more than five-fold increase in emissions over this twenty-year growth cycle, assuming growth is fueled primarily by oil, coal, and natural gas.

The United States can hardly lecture Indonesia about emissions as a byproduct of economic growth. Still, if Indonesia and other emerging economies grow on the basis of a fossil-fuel dominated energy infrastructure, the chance of achieving the IPCC's global emissions reduction target would be close to zero. But, as we have seen in Chapter 5, if Indonesia invests about 1.5 percent of GDP in energy efficiency and clean renewables every year over the next 20 years, emissions per capita would stabilize at the country's current low level, even as the economy grows at around 6 percent per year. The expansion in employment opportunities would also be substantial, as we saw in Chapter 6.

The Fight against Fossil Fuel Companies

We have concerned ourselves with the costs the clean energy transition would take on workers and communities dependent on the fossil fuel industry. But what about the fossil fuel companies? There is no escaping the fact that they will experience major losses. How should we address this issue?

As a first step, we need to have a clear grasp of the scale of the losses that fossil fuel asset owners are likely to face. A 2013 study published jointly by Carbon Tracker and the Grantham Institute on Climate Change and the Environment at the London School of Economics examined the current holdings of the largest 200 private-sector fossil fuel companies, as listed in the world's various stock exchanges. This study estimated that "60–80 percent of coal, oil, and gas reserves of [these] firms are unburnable." The study then considered the implications of this finding for the long-term valuations for these companies. They conclude that "The 200 fossil fuel companies analyzed here have a market value of $4 trillion and debt of $1.5 trillion. . . . Equity valuations could be reduced by 40–60 percent in a low emissions scenario. In parallel, the bonds of fossil fuel companies could also be vulnerable to ratings downgrades."[2] As a rough estimate working from these figures, we are looking at around $3 trillion in lost value for these companies over the next twenty years, and the certainty of further declines subsequently.

As I stated in Chapter 1, these companies are obviously not about to relinquish $3 trillion in wealth without a fight. They will present the most serious forces of opposition to an effective global clean energy project. In the United States, the political activities of David and Charles Koch illustrate the situation well. The Koch brothers are the majority owners of Koch Industries, the second largest privately held corporation in the United States, whose most important businesses are within various fossil fuel sectors. As of 2014, their combined personal net worth was around $80 billion. For many years, they have been financing—at unprecedented levels—publications and political action around climate change skepticism as well as other right-wing causes. For the 2014 U.S. election cycle, they mobilized $300 million to advance their political agenda.[3] For the 2016 election cycle, they plan to spend $900 million, which would put their operation at rough financial parity with both the Democratic and Republican presidential candidates.[4] The Koch brothers are clearly not prepared to be swayed by the scientific consensus on climate change.

We should expect that such forms of resistance will only intensify as the global clean energy project gathers force. At the same time, overstating how much the private fossil fuel companies have at stake does not help matters. Without question, $3 trillion is a huge sum of money. But, as of 2012, it equals only 1.3 percent of the $225 trillion in total worldwide private financial assets—the total value of all equity and debt assets outstanding.[5] Still more, the anticipated $3 trillion decline in the value of private fossil fuel assets will not happen in one fell swoop, but rather will occur incrementally over a twenty-year period. On average, this amounts to asset losses of $150 billion per year. By contrast, as a result of the U.S. housing bubble and subsequent financial collapse in 2007–09, U.S. homeowners lost $16 trillion in asset values in 2008 alone—about 100 times the annual losses fossil fuel companies would face.

The fact that the decline in fossil fuel asset values will occur incrementally over decades also means that asset holders will have ample opportunity to diversify their holdings. Many are already doing so. As one important example, in June 2014 Warren Buffet, the best-known investor and third richest person in the world, announced that his holding company Berkshire Hathaway was doubling its holdings in solar and wind energy companies to $15 billion. This is even while Berkshire continues to hold large positions in conventional utility companies.[6]

On another track, since 2013, there has been a rapidly growing global movement for a wide range of organizations to divest themselves of their fossil fuel asset holdings. The divestment movement includes foundations, universities, religious organizations, and municipalities located throughout the United States and Western Europe as well as Canada, South Africa, Australia, and New Zealand. As of this writing, nearly 200 organizations have sold off roughly $50 billion in fossil fuel assets. Some examples of the organizations involved thus far include, in the United States, Stanford University, the New School, the University of Dayton, Hampshire College, the Rockefeller Brothers Fund, and the cities of Providence, Rhode Island and Ithaca, New York; in Europe, the Universities of Glasgow and Bedfordshire, Chalmers University of Technology in Sweden, and the cities of Oslo, Norway, Oxford, United Kingdom, and Orebro, Sweden; and in

New Zealand and Australia, Victoria University and the cities of Moreland, Fremantle, and Dunedin.[7]

The divestment movement offers great promise. It is likely to become a growing force in reshaping investor attitudes toward fossil fuel companies. But thus far, the movement is missing half the equation because it is focused only on relinquishing fossil fuel stocks. It needs to become just as actively committed to *reinvestment* in clean energy enterprises. To push global CO_2 emissions down by 40 percent within twenty years, it is imperative that energy efficiency and clean renewable investments expand at least as rapidly as fossil fuel operations contract.

Nevertheless, the divestment movement is already demonstrating that major amounts of money can be effectively moved out of the fossil fuel industry regardless of what the Koch brothers or other defenders of the status quo may think about the matter. The overarching point is that the fossil fuel industry will have to experience major contractions over the next two decades, and, over the longer term, near-total demise. There is no choice in the matter if we take seriously, as we must, the research produced by climate scientists. The profits of oil, coal, and natural gas companies will simply have to yield to the imperative of sustaining life on earth.

Appendix 1: Estimating Global Costs for Expanding Clean Renewable Energy Productive Capacity

As noted in the main text, the International Renewable Energy Agency (IRENA) presents figures on total costs of generating electricity from alternative renewable energy sources throughout all regions of the world.[1] The U.S. Energy Agency (EIA), a branch of the U.S. Energy Department, provides similar figures on electricity generating costs for the U.S. economy. As my co-authors and I show (Pollin 2015a), these respective electricity cost estimates from IRENA and EIA are broadly similar, despite the fact that the EIA's figures are for the U.S. only and the IRENA figures encompass all regions of the world. At the same time, the EIA's figures provide much greater detail than those from IRENA in breaking down the components of overall costs.

Given the similarities in the overall cost figures, it is reasonable to use the detailed figures from the U.S. to derive rough estimates on specifically the average investment expenditures necessary to expand clean renewable capacity by a given amount—e.g. 1 Q-BTU—over our twenty-year investment period. As I state in the main text, that rough cost estimate is $230 billion to expand capacity by 1 Q-BTU. I have derived that figure based on the following data and calculations.

In Table A1.1, to begin with, I report figures from the EIA on the present value of capital expenditure costs estimates for building renewable energy capacity in the U.S. The table shows two sets of figures from the EIA: a Reference case set of costs as of 2017 and a Low-Cost Technology case as of 2035. Under the Low-Cost Technology case, the EIA assumes that costs will fall by 40 percent relative to the 2017 Reference case for all renewables other than hydro. It assumes no cost reductions for hydro over this period. As the table shows, in the EIA's 2017 reference case, the present value of capital expenditures ranges between $207 per Q-BTU with bioenergy to $521 billion with solar PV. Under the Low Cost Renewable Technology case, the range is between $124 and $312 billion per Q-BTU.

Working from these EIA figures, we then estimate the average costs over a twenty-year investment cycle. Table A1.2 shows the relevant calculations. I first assume that the average costs for

Table A1.1 U.S. Capital Expenditure Costs for Building Renewable Electricity Capacity
Figures are present values of total capital costs per Q-BTU of capacity

	2017 Reference Case	2035 Low Cost Technology Case Assumes 40% cost reduction except for hydro
Bioenergy	$207 billion	$124 billion
Hydro	$284 billion	$284 billion
Onshore Wind	$306 billion	$183 billion
Solar PV	$521 billion	$312 billion
Geothermal	$285 billion	$167 billion

Source: Author's calculations based on primary source presented in Pollin et al. (2014), pp. 135-37.

each of the clean renewable energy sources will be the midpoint between the 2017 Reference case figure and the 2025 Low-Cost Renewable Technology case. I show those midpoint figures in column 2 of Table A1.2. I then assume that, over the twenty-year investment cycle, the extent of investments in each of the clean renewable sources will break down as follows: 50 percent of total investments for clean bioenergy, and 12.5 percent each for small-scale hydro, onshore wind, solar photovoltaic, and geothermal. I assume the high proportional investment figure for clean bioenergy over the twenty-year period precisely because it will remain as the low-cost source of clean renewable energy.

Based on our midpoint figures column 2 and the assumptions on the distribution of capital expenditures by clean renewable source in column 3, I then show in column 4 of Table A1.2 a weighted capital expenditure cost figure per Q-BTU of capacity expansion. As we see in the last row of column 4, that weighted cost figure is $229.2 billion.

Table A1.2 Estimated Global Average Capital Expenditure Costs for Clean Renewable Energy Expansion over 20-Year Investment Cycle

1) Sector	2) Estimated costs for expanding productive capacity by 1 Q-BTU *(in billions USD)*	3) Assumptions of capital expenditure expansion over 20-year investment cycle	4) Weighted capital expenditure costs per Q-BTU of capacity expansion
Clean bioenergy	$165 billion	50.0%	$83 billion
Hydro	$284 billion	12.5%	$35.3 billion
Onshore wind	$245 billion	12.5%	$30.6 billion
Solar photovoltaic	$417 billion	12.5%	$52.1 billion
Geothermal	$226 billion	12.5%	$28.2 billion
Weighted Average Costs	---	---	$229.2 billion

Sources: See Table A1.1 and description of calculations in Appendix 1 text.

Appendix 2: Model for Estimating Global CO_2 Reductions through 20-Year Clean Energy Investment Program

In Chapter 5, I present the key assumptions through which I generate the results presented in Tables 5.1 and 5.2 as well Figures 5.1 through 5.3. In this appendix, I show the steps through which I derived the results reported in Chapter 5.

Global Model Framework and Calculations

We begin with the estimates presented in Table A2.1 (p.126). As we see, we start with the actual global GDP figure in 2013 of \$75 trillion.[1] Working from this figure, we then work with our assumption of global GDP growth over the subsequent twenty years at 3.4 percent per year. From our initial 2013 GDP figure of \$75 trillion and our assumption of 3.4 percent growth, we can then estimate the level of GDP every year over the next twenty years. As shown in Table A2.1, we can also then calculate the "midrange" GDP figure over the twenty-year investment cycle. I define the midrange figure as being equal to the average of the actual 2013 GDP figure and our estimate of GDP in 2033. This midrange figure, as we see, is \$112 trillion. From this midrange figure, we can then readily calculate an average figure for average annual clean renewable investments.

Table A2.1 Twenty-year Spending Trajectory for Clean Renewables and Energy Efficiency Investments

2013 Global GDP	$75 trillion
Projected 20-year average annual GDP growth rate *(from IEA, 2014)*	3.4%
Projected 2033 GDP *(with 3.4 % average annual GDP growth)*	$150 trillion
Midrange GDP value for investment spending estimates *(= (2013 GDP + 2033 GDP)/2)*	$112 trillion
Average annual clean renewable investments *(= 1.0% of midrange GDP)*	$1.1 trillion
Average annual energy efficiency investments *(= 0.5% of midrange GDP)*	$550 billion

Sources: International Monetary Fund, World Economic Outlook Database 2015, IEA (2014).

At 1 percent of annual GDP, that average annual clean renewable investment figure is $1.1 trillion. We make similar calculations for average annual energy efficiency investments. As Table A2.1 shows, our average annual energy efficiency figure, at 0.5 percent of the midrange global GDP, is $550 billion.

In Table A2.2, I then present the calculations through which, over the full twenty-year investment cycle, I estimate the extent of both clean renewable capacity expansion as well as the savings generated through energy efficiency investments. We begin with the estimates of the average costs for achieving clean energy capacity expansions and energy efficiency gains. That is, as we see in Table A2.2, we assume an average cost for clean renewables capacity expansion of $200 billion per Q-BTU of capacity, and $30 billion per Q-BTU, on average, for energy efficiency gains.

Our full investment cycle is twenty years, but, as noted in the main text, we are assuming that there will be, on average, a three-year delay before the investment project is operating at full scale on a global basis. To account for this delay factor, I assume that the investment cycle is, in practice, only seventeen years, not twenty

Table A2.2 Cost Assumptions and Capacity Expansion for
Clean Renewables and Energy Efficiency Investments

	Clean Renewable Energy	Energy Efficiency
1) Cost Assumptions	$200 billion per Q-BTU of Capacity	$30 billion per Q-BTU of energy savings
2) Total Spending with 17-Year Spending Cycle (= row 1 x 17)	$18.7 trillion	$9.3 trillion
3) Total Capacity Expansion or Energy Savings through 17-Year Spending Cycle (= row 2/row 1)	93.5 Q-BTUs	310 Q- BTUs

Source: Cost assumptions for clean renewable energy in Chapter 4 and Appendix 1;
cost assumptions for energy efficiency in Chapter 3.

years. Investing an average of $1.1 trillion per year in clean renew-
able capacity and $550 billion in energy efficiency will therefore
generate, as we show in row 2 of Table A2.2, $18.7 trillion in clean
renewable investments and $9.3 trillion in energy efficiency invest-
ments. From these figures, we then see in row 3 the total capacity
expansion or energy savings through the 17-year spending cycle—
i.e. 93.5 Q-BTUs of new clean renewable productive capacity and
310 Q-BTUs of energy savings through efficiency investments.

Table A2.3 (p. 128) shows how, relative to the IEA's Current
Policies Scenario, the 93.5 Q-BTUs in clean renewable expansion
and 310 Q-BTUs in energy efficiency savings impacts 1) total
global energy consumption; 2) total clean renewable supply; 3)
total residual demand for fossil fuels; 4) total global CO_2 emissions; and 5) total CO_2 emissions per capita. As rows 5 and 6
of Table 2.3 show, the overall impact the clean energy investment program will be to lower global CO_2 emissions from the
IEA's estimate of 43 billion metric tons to 20 billion metric tons.
Global average CO_2 emissions per capita similarly fall from 4.9
metric tons per capita to 2.3 tons per capita.

Table A2.3 Impact of Clean Energy Investment Program Relative to International Energy Agency "Current Policies" Scenario for 2035

	IEA Current Policies Scenario *(IEA 2014)*	20-year Clean Energy Investment Scenario
1. Total Energy Consumptionin Q-BTUs	754 Q- BTUs	444 Q- BTUs *(= 754 – 310 BTUs in energy efficiency savings)*
2. Total Clean Renewable Energy Supply	40 Q- BTUs	133.5 Q- BTUs *(93.5 + 40 Q-BTUs)*
3. Total Nuclear Power Supply	40 Q-BTUs	25 Q-BTUs
4. Total Fossil Fuel + High-Emissions Renewables	764 Q- BTUs	286 Q-BTUs
5. Total CO_2 Emissions *(in metric tons)*	43 billion	20 billion *(= 286 Q-BTUs × .07 billion tons/Q-BTU*
6. Total CO_2 Emissions per capita *(with population = 8.7billion)*	4.9	2.3

Sources: Tables A2.1, A2.2 and IEA 2014.

Assumptions for Individual Country Estimates

Table A2.4 presents the main assumptions underlying the country-specific estimates of per capita CO_2 emissions presented in Chapter 5. The GDP growth assumptions listed in column 1 of Table A2.4 come directly from IEA (2014) for Brazil, China, India, South Africa and the U.S. The figures for Germany, Indonesia, and South Korea are presented in Chapters 9, 10, and 12 respectively of Pollin et al. (2015a). The figures on Spain are presented in Pollin et al. (2015c).

Column 2 of Table A2.4 lists my assumptions as to the share of annual GDP that will be channeled into clean energy

Table A2.4 Main Assumptions underlying Individual Country Estimates on CO_2 Emissions Reductions *(7/13/15 version)*

	1) Average annual 20-year GDP growth rate	2) Increased clean energy investment spending as share of GDP	3) Average costs to raise energy efficiency levels by 1 Q-BTU	Average costs to expand clean renewable capacity by 1 Q-BTU
Brazil	3.4%	1.0%	$20 billion	$200 billion
China	5.0%	1.0%	$20 billion	$200 billion
Germany	2.0%	1.0%	See references in Pollin et al. (2015a), Chapter 9	
India	6.0%	1.5%	$20 billion	$200 billion
Indonesia	5.0%	1.5%	$20 billion	$200 billion
South Africa	4.0%	1.5%	$20 billion	$200 billion
South Korea	3.3%	1.5%	$20 billion	$200 billion
Spain	2.4%	1.5%	$30 billion	$200 billion
United States	2.1%	1.0%	$30 billion	$200 billion

Sources: Pollin et al. (2014), (2015a), (2015b), and (2015c). Additional supplemental modeling and results, especially on China, available from author.

investments relative to the IEA's BAU model. As we see, for Brazil, China, Germany and the United States, I assume that the annual current increase totals 1 percent of GDP, while the figure is 1.5 percent for the other five countries. The reason I assume the lower proportional spending figures for Brazil, China, Germany and the U.S. differ by country.

Brazil, to begin with, is already a very strong performer it terms of CO_2 emissions, at 2.3 tons per capita. This is half the current world average of 4.6 tons, while Brazil is still producing domestic output at an upper-middle income level. At the same time, Brazil is unique in that its share of total greenhouse gas emissions generated by CO_2 is substantially less than the world average. This is not only because Brazil relies more heavily on hydro power, thereby reducing the share of emissions that would otherwise result through generating electricity by burning fossil fuels. The less favorable factor here is that Brazil generates high levels of methane and nitrous oxide emissions from deforestation of the Amazon and the corresponding growth of agriculture. It would therefore be appropriate for Brazil to devote a relatively high share of its overall GDP on controlling methane and nitrous oxide emissions while allowing that a somewhat smaller 1.0 percent of GDP be channeled into pushing CO_2 emissions down beyond the already low level.[2]

Among high-income economies, Germany is, similar to Brazil, a very strong performer in terms of controlling CO_2 emissions. The country has also already established a highly ambitious program over the next twenty years—the *Energiewende*—to achieve further emission reductions. The assumptions I report for Germany on clean energy investments at roughly 1 percent of GDP above the government's own BAU assumptions, as well as for costs, and emissions reductions themselves, are derived directly from the German government's own *Energy Concept* document.[3]

There are a few interrelated reasons as to why I have assumed that annual clean energy investments for China and the U.S. would be 1.0 rather than 1.5 percent of GDP greater than the amounts incorporated into the IEA's BAU framework. The first is that since the absolute levels of GDP in both countries are very high, the absolute expansion of clean energy investments would be correspondingly high, even at 1.0 rather than 1.5 percent of GDP. It therefore may not be realistic to expect the absolute investment levels to expand much faster, or, similarly, to realistically expect CO_2 emissions in both countries to fall significantly beyond the 54–60 percent range that I have derived from the models with a 1 percent share of GDP increase channeled into clean energy investments. This is especially true given that, relative to the global average, both countries are already at the high end of clean energy investment spending as a share of GDP.

At the same time, if we assuming that China and the U.S. could be channeling a somewhat lower share of their respective GDPs into domestic clean energy investments, it also reasonable to expect both countries to provide generous financial support on a large scale to other countries' clean energy investment programs. Such financial support will help enable these other countries to sustain their clean energy investment programs at a level that is at 1.5 percent of GDP or above relative to the BAU assumptions for these economies.

Column 3 of Table A2.4 shows my assumptions for each country on the average costs of achieving a gain in energy efficiency by 1 Q-BTU over the full 20-year investment cycle. As I discussed in Chapter 3, a significant part of the large overall differences in cost estimates for energy efficiency savings, as reported in Table 3.2, is differences in labor costs between countries. Given this, I assume that the costs of efficiency gains will average $20 billion per Q-BTU for countries with relatively low labor costs, including Brazil, China, Indonesia, South Africa, and South Korea. For two of the high-income countries in our sample of 9—Spain, and the U.S.—I assume that the cost of efficiency gains will average $30 billion per Q-BTU of savings. The German cost figures are embedded in the government's own *Energy Concept* framework

Finally, column 4 of Table A2.4 shows my assumption on average costs over the 20-year investment cycle for expanding productive capacity for clean renewable energy sources by 1 Q-BTU. As we see, we assume that average figure to be $200 per Q-BTU for all countries (again, with the exception of Germany, in which we have again derived estimates directly from the *Energy Concept* document). In Appendix 1, I discussed how I derived that average figure for all countries.

Notes

1   Introduction: The Global Green Energy Challenge

1. Expressed in Celsius temperature units, stabilization will need to occur at about 2 degrees above the pre-industrial global mean temperature of around 13.72 degrees Celsius.

2. I am relying on three main sources for data on global CO_2 and overall greenhouse gas emissions: the U.S. Energy Information Agency's (EIA) *International Energy Statistics*, the International Energy Agency's (IEA) *World Energy Outlook*, and the World Bank's *World Development Indicators*. There are small differences in details among these three sources. To reconcile these differences, I have tried to use the source that provides the most recent set of figures for a full sample of countries. I have used less recent data, as needed, when they provide an improved level of detail. Most importantly, I have used the World Bank figures on overall greenhouse gas and CO_2 emissions, since they provide the greatest level of detail on this critical matter, including detailed figures on other greenhouse gas sources other than CO_2. Thus, as of July, 2015, the World Bank Indicators online site reports that, as of 2010, total global greenhouse gas emissions were at 44.9 billion tons, and CO_2 emissions were at 33.5 billion tons. The EIA online site reports that, as of 2012, total global CO_2 emissions were at 32.3 billion tons, but in March 2015 had reported 32.7 for 2012 emissions. IEA (2014, p. 608) reports that, as of 2012, global CO_2 emissions were at 31.6 billion tons, but projects that figure rising to 34.2 billion tons as of 2020. As a workable midpoint

figure, I assume throughout this study that 2012 global CO_2 emissions were at 32.7 billion tons. Working from this midpoint figure, I then have made small adjustments throughout to harmonize data from the three sources.

3. Both the EIA and IEA report all CO_2 emissions as coming from oil, coal and natural gas, even though both organizations also recognize that high-emissions bioenergy sources generate CO_2 emissions at equivalent levels as coal and oil. It is common to combine the CO_2 emissions from renewable energy sources with those from burning fossil fuels. I will follow that convention in reporting overall emissions levels. But I will also devote attention to the issues around high-emissions renewables themselves.

4. According to the World Bank's *World Development Indicators*, the total of 44.9 billion tons of greenhouse gas emissions as of 2012 consisted in full of: 33.5 billion tons of CO_2 emissions from combusting fossil fuels (75 percent of total); 7.5 billion tons of methane produced both energy generation and agriculture (17 percent of total); 2.9 billion tons of nitrous oxide generated through a combination of energy, industry and agricultural production (6 percent of total); and byproduct emissions of hydrofluorocarbons, perfluorocarbons, and sulfur hexafluoride. See http://wdi.worldbank.org/table/3.9.

5. See Nemet et al. (2010) and Boyce and Pastor (2013) on these additional environmental and health "co-benefits" of reducing CO_2 emissions.

6. The figure on global renewable energy investments is from the Frankfurt School-UNEP Collaborating Centre's report *Global Trends in Renewable Energy Investment 2014, Key Findings*, p. 11. The figures on global energy efficiency investments is from the International Energy Agency's 2013 *Energy Efficiency Market Report*, pp. 47–50. The IEA study provides an extensive methological discussion on the challenges involved in "measuring the market for energy efficiency," (Chapter 2 of study). Through this discussion, they do nevertheless conclude that "the IEA estimates that total global investment in energy efficiency measures in

2011 was up to USD 300 billion" (p. 49). But they also provide, as a range, $147–$300 billion (p. 47).

7. See Leaton et al. (2013). More generally, Carbon Tracker has also produced a useful series of studies that are available on their website.

8. IEA (2014), p. 687. The tables in this IEA study showing their alternative projections are on pp. 608-09. The figures I report for 2035 for the Current Policies and 450 scenarios are midpoints between their 2030 and 2040 estimates.

9. Among high-income economies, the countries with higher per capita energy consumption rates are Canada, Finland, Luxembourg, and Norway.

10. These categories are: "low income" countries, with average per capita income at $632; "lower-middle income" countries, with average per capita income at $2,355; "upper-middle Income" countries, with average per capita income at $7,650; and "high income" countries, with average per capita income at $38,133.

2 Prospects for Fossil Fuels and Nuclear Power

1. See Jackson et al. 2011, pp. 3-4, as well as the follow-up 2013 study by Jackson and co-authors.

2. See references in Romm (2014) at http://thinkprogress.org/climate/2014/10/22/3582904/methane-leaks-climate-benefit-fracking/.

3. See Romm (2008).

4. IEA 2013a, p. 53.

5. See EIA website, "Nuclear Explained: Nuclear Power and the Environment," http://www.eia.gov/energyexplained/index.cfm?page=nuclear_environment.

6. Miller and Sagan (2009), p. 10. This article introduces the full two-volume special issue of *Daedalus* (Fall 2009/Winter 2010) on nuclear proliferation.

7. Takenaka and Topham 2013.

8. IEO 2013, p. 95.

3 Prospects for Energy Efficiency

1. 2010, p. 5561.

2. McKinsey (2010). McKinsey has published a series of additional reports on the gains available from energy efficiency investments.

3. 2010, pp. 4-5.

4. See the 2010 BMUB (German Federal Ministry for the Environment, Nature Conservation, and Nuclear Safety) study.

5. See the discussion in Pollin et al. 2015, Chapter 4, which includes full references on the Jevons book and other references on the rebound effect.

6. Government of India (2006), p. 83.

4 Prospects for Clean Renewable Energy

1. *Global Trends in Renewable Energy Investments 2014 Key Findings*, p. 11, at http://www.unep.org/pdf/Green_energy_2013-Key_findings.pdf.

2. IRENA (2012). The IRENA website is, more generally, a valuable resource of data and analysis on global renewable energy developments.

3. See Pollin et al. (2014) for further discussion on this issue.

4. Kosnik (2010) p. 5512.

5. Sargsyan et al. (2010), p. 18.

6. Baker (2014), p. 78.

7. *Bloomberg Sustainable Energy Factbook* 2013, p. 3 at http://about.bnef.com/white-papers/sustainable-energy-in-america-2013-factbook/.

8. Trabish (2013).

9. IEA (2014), pp. 317–18.

5   How to Hit the CO_2 Emissions Reduction Target

1. I am assuming that under the IEA's BAU case for 2035, global clean energy investments remain at between 0.2–0.3 percent of global GDP, though the IEA does not state this explicitly.

2. This observation is frequently attributed inaccurately to the late John Kenneth Galbraith.

3. I have made some adjustments in assumptions on an individual country basis, given the specific conditions within each of the countries. I describe these adjustments in Appendix 2.

6   Expanding Job Opportunities

1. See Chapter 6 and Appendix 3 of Pollin et al. (2015a) for a full discussion of the employment estimating methodology used here.

2. Germany, South Korea and Spain do all have small oil refining sectors, even though they are not oil producers. Jobs will be lost in these sectors as clean energy production increasingly supplant imported oil as an energy source. However, these oil refining job losses should be largely counterbalanced through an increase in bioenergy refining activity—i.e. producing clean-burning ethanol from agricultural wastes and switchgrass.

3. Strietska-Ilina et al. (2011), p. 100.

4. Renner et al. (2008), p. 27.

5. Mazzocchi (1993), p. 41. See also Leopold's outstanding 2007 biography of Mazzocchi for the historical context on the issues of a Superfund for workers and just transition.

7   A Policy Agenda That Can Work

1. (2006), p. 172, emphasis in original.

2. (2014), p. 136.

3. Cory, Couture, and Kreycik (2009), p. 2.

4. IEA (2013b), p. 149.

5. Taylor et al. (2008).

6. (2013), p. 6.

7. Amsden (2001), p.127, emphasis in original.

8. Bollinger's 2001 and 2005 are both valuable studies on this question.

9. *Financial Times*, 1/13/15, http://www.ft.com/intl/cms/s/0/b411852e-9b05-11e4-882d-00144feabdc0.html#axzz3gJfvRdyM

10. (2013), p. 227.

11. This section follows closely from Pollin et al. (2015a), pp. 120-121, and Pollin et al (2015c).

12. In Pollin et al. (2015b), we discuss in depth the major advantages Spain can achieve through reducing its oil import dependency, especially as the country attempts to work its way out of the severe recession and austerity conditions that have prevailed there since the 2007-09 global financial collapse.

13. Influential "de-growth" positions are presented in Victor (2008), Jackson (2009), Schor (2010), and D'Alisa (2015).

8   Risk, Ethics, and the Politics of Climate Stabilization

1. Retrieved from http://cdiac.ornl.gov/trends/emis/tre_tp20.html#.

2. The quotes in this paragraph are from Leaton et al. (2013), pp. 4-5.

3. Retrieved from http://www.thedailybeast.com/articles/2014/06/13/koch-brothers-make-climate-activists-new-target.html.

4. Retrieved from http://www.nytimes.com/2015/01/27/us/politics/kochs-plan-to-spend-900-million-on-2016-campaign.html.

5. Retrieved from http://www.mckinsey.com/insights/global_capital_markets/financial_globalization.

6. Retrieved from http://www.bloomberg.com/news/articles/2014-06-10/buffett-ready-to-double-15-billion-solar-wind-bet.

7. http://gofossilfree.org/commitments/.

Appendix 1   Estimating Global Costs

1. Total costs for electricity generation are typically calculated in terms of "levelized costs of electricity," or LCOE. Levelized costs represent the per-kilowatt hour or (per-Q-BTU) cost, adjusted for inflation, of building and operating a generating plant over an assumed financial life and duty cycle. Key inputs to calculating levelized costs include overnight capital costs, fuel costs, fixed and variable operations and maintenance (O&M) costs, financing costs, and an assumed utilization rate for each plant type.

Appendix 2   Model for Estimating Global CO_2 Reduction

1. This $75 trillion global GDP figure is based on the prevailing exchange rates between the U.S. and all other global currencies as of 2013. The most widely utilized alternative measure of global GDP is derived through establishing purchasing power parities between countries—that is, how much of an overall basket of goods and services one can purchase in any given country, measured in U.S. dollars. Global GDP in 2013, measured according to the purchasing power parity methodology, was $87 billion. I have quoted this higher global GDP figure in the main text because it is generally regarded as more accurate for understanding the level of economic activity occurring within each country. However, for the purposes of this exercise, it is important to, if anything, err by underestimating the prospects for a clean energy investment program over the 20-year investment cycle. Therefore, for this exercise, I utilize the lower $75 trillion figure derived on the basis of exchange rates as of 2013.

2. See Pollin et al. (2015a) Chapter 8 for further discussion on the Brazil case.

3. See Pollin et al. (2015a) Chapter 9 for further discussion on the German case.

References

Amsden, Alice H. (2001) *The Rise of "The Rest": Challenges to the West from Late-Industrializing Economies*. New York, NY: Oxford University Press.

Baker, J. Mark (2014) "Small Hydropower Development in Himachal Pradesh: An Analysis of Socioecological Effects," *Economic & Political Weekly*, May 24, pp. 77–86.

Bolinger, Mark A. (2001) *Community Wind Power Ownership Schemes in Europe and their Relevance to the United States*, Berkeley, CA: Ernest Orlando Lawrence Berkeley National Laboratory.

Bolinger, Mark A. (2005) Making European-style Community Wind Power Development Work in the US. *Renewable and Sustainable Energy Reviews*, 9(6), pp. 556–575.

Boyce, James K. and Manuel Pastor (2013) "Clearing the air: incorporating air quality and environmental justice into climate policy" *Climatic Change*, August.

BMUB (German Federal Ministry for the Environment, Nature Conservation, and Nuclear Safety), 2010. *Energy Concept for an Environmentally Sound, Reliable and Affordable Energy Supply*. Berlin.

Cory, Karlynn, Toby Couture, and Claire Kreycik. (2009) "Feed-in Tariff Policy: Design, Implementation, and RPS Policy Interactions." Golden,

CO: National Renewable Energy Laboratory. Available at http://www.
nrel.gov/docs/fy09osti/45549.pdf.

D'Alisa, Giacomo, Frederico Demaria and Giorgos Kallis (2015) *Degrowth: A Vocabulary for a New Era*, New York: Routledge.

Emanuel, Kerry (2012) *What We Know About Climate Change*. Boston Review Books. Cambridge, MA: MIT Press. 2nd edition.

EIA (U.S. Energy Information Administration) (2015) *Nuclear Explained: Nuclear Power and the Environment*. Available at: <www.eia.gov/energyex-plained/index.cfm?page=nuclear_environment> (Accessed July 2015).

EIA (U.S. Energy Information Administration) (2013) *International Energy Outlook 2013*. Washington, DC.

EIA (U.S. Energy Information Administration) (2015) *International Energy Statistics*. Available at: http://www.eia.gov/cfapps/ipdbproject/IEDIn-dex3.cfm (Accessed July 2015).

Frankfurt School-UNEP Collaborating Centre and Bloomberg New Energy Finance, 2014. *Global Trends in Renewable Energy Investment 2014*. Frankfurt: Frankfurt School of Finance & Management.

Government of India (2006) *Integrated Energy Policy: Report of the Expert Committee*. Planning Commission, New Delhi.

IEA (International Energy Agency) (2013a) *World Energy Outlook 2013*. Paris: OECD/IEA.

IEA (2013b) *Energy Efficiency Market Report 2013: Market Trends and Medium Term Prospects*. Paris: OECD/IEA (International Energy Agency), 2014. *World Energy Outlook 2014*. Paris: OECD/IEA.

IRENA (International Renewable Energy Agency) (2013) *Renewable Power Generation Costs in 2012: An Overview*. Abu Dhabi.

Jackson, Robert B., Brooks R. Pearson, Stephen G. Osborn, Nathanel R. Warner, and Avner Vengosh (2011) *Research and Policy Recommendations for Hydraulic Fracturing and Shale-Gas Extraction*. Durham, NC: Center on Global Change, Duke University.

Jackson, Robert B., Avner Vengosh, Thomas H. Darrah, Nathanel R. Warner, Adrian Down, Robert J. Poreda, Stephen G. Osborn, Kaiguang Zhao and Jonathan D. Karr (2013) *Increased Stray Gas Abundance in a Subset of Drinking Water Wells Near Marcellus Shale Gas Extraction*. Washington, DC: Proceedings of the National Academy of Sciences.

Jackson, Tim (2009) *Prosperity without Growth: Economics for a Finite Planet*, London: Earthscan.

Jevons, William S. (1865) *The Coal Question*. London: MacMillan and Co.

Kosnik, Lea (2010) "The Potential for Small Scale Hydropower Development in the U.S." *Energy Policy* 38 (10): 5512–5519.

Leaton, James, Nicola Ranger, Bob Ward, Luke Sussams, and Meg Brown (2013) *Unburnable Carbon 2013: Wasted Capital and Stranded Assets*, London, Carbon Tracker and the Grantham Research Institute, London School of Economics, http://www.lse.ac.uk/GranthamInstitute/wp-content/uploads/2014/02/PB-unburnable-carbon-2013-wasted-capital-stranded-assets.pdf (Accessed July 2015).

Leopold, Les (2007) *The Man Who Hated Work and Loved Labor: The Life and Times of Tony Mazzocchi*. White River Junction, VT: Chelsea Green Publishing Company.

Li, Wen., Janine Birmele, Harald Schaich, and Werner Konold, (2013) "Transitioning to Community-Owned Renewable Energy: Lessons from Germany," *Procedia Environmental Sciences*, 17, pp. 719-728.

Mazzocchi, Tony (1993) "A Superfund for Workers," *Earth Island Journal*, 9(1), pp. 40-41.

Mazzucato, Mariana (2013) *The Entrepreneurial State: Debunking Public vs. Private Sector Myths*. New York, NY: Anthem Press.

McKinsey & Company, (2010a) *Energy Efficiency: A Compelling Global Resource*. New York, NY.

NAS (National Academy of Sciences), NAE (National Academy of Engineering), and NRC (National Research Council) (2010) 2010. *Real Pros-*

pects for Energy Efficiency in the United States. Washington, DC: National Academies Press.

Miller, Steven E. and Scott D. Sagan (2009) "Nuclear Power without Nuclear Proliferation?" *Daedalus*, Fall, pp. 7–18.

Nemet G.F., T. Holloway and P. Meier (2010) "Implications of Incorporating Air-Quality Co-benefits into Climate Change Policymaking," *Environmental Research Letters* 5(1).

Pollin, Robert., Heidi Garrett-Peltier, James Heintz, and Bracken Hendricks (2014) *Green Growth: A U.S. Program for Controlling Climate Change and Expanding Job Opportunities*. Washington, DC: Center for American Progress, https://cdn.americanprogress.org/wp-content/uploads/2014/09/PERI.pdf.

Pollin, Robert, Heidi Garrett-Peltier, James Heintz, and Shouvik Chakraborty (2015a) *Global Green Growth: Clean Energy Industrial Investments and Expanding Job Opportunities,* United Nations Industrial Development Organization and Global Green Growth Institute, http://gggi.org/wp-content/uploads/2015/06/GGGI-VOL-I_WEB.pdf.

Pollin, Robert and Shouvik Chakraborty (2015b) "An Egalitarian Green Growth Program for India," PERI Working Paper #389.

Pollin, Robert, Heidi Garrett-Peltier, and Shouvik Chakraborty (2015c) "A Clean Energy Investment Program for Spain," Amherst, MA: PERI Working Paper #390.

Renner, Michael. Sean Sweeney, and Jill Kubit (2008) *Green Jobs: Toward Decent Work in a Sustainable, Low-Carbon World*. Nairobi: United Nations Environmental Program.

Romm, Joe (2008) *Is Coal With Carbon Capture and Storage a Core Climate Solution?* Climate Progress. Available at: http://thinkprogress.org/climate/2008/09/29/203149/is-coal-with-carbon-capture-and-storage-a-core-climatesolution/ (Accessed July 2015).

Ruttan, Vernon W. (2006) *Is War Necessary for Economic Growth? Military Procurement and Technology Development*.New York, NY: Oxford University Press.

Sarkar, Ashok and Jas Singh (2010) "Financing Energy Efficiency in Developing Countries – Lessons Learned and Remaining Challenges," *Energy Policy*, 38(10), pp. 5560-5571.

Sargsyan, Gevorg, Mikul Bhatia, Sudeshna Ghosh Banerjee, Krishnan Raghunathan, and Ruchi Soni (2010) *Unleashing the Potential of Renewable Energy in India*, South Asia Energy Unit, Sustainable Development Department, The World Bank, https://openknowledge.worldbank.org/bitstream/handle/10986/2318/627060PUB0Unle000public00BOX3614 89B.pdf?sequence=1.

Schor, Juliet (2010) Plenitude: *The New Economics of True Wealth*, New York: The Penguin Press.

Spratt, Stephen, Stephanie Griffith-Jones and Jose Antonio (2013) *Mobilising Investment for Inclusive Green Growth in Low-Income Countries*. Berlin: Deutsche Gesselllschaft fur Internationale Zusammenarbeit, http://www.stephanygj.net/papers/MobilisingInvestmentforInclusiveGreen-Growth2013.pdf.

Strietska-Ilina, Olga, Christine Hofmann, Mercedes D. Haro and Shinyoung Jeon, S (2011) *Skills for Green Jobs: A Global View*. Geneva: International Labour Office, http://www.ilo.org/wcmsp5/groups/public/---dgreports/---dcomm/---publ/documents/publication/wcms_159585.pdf.

Takenaka, Kyoshi and James Topham (2013) *Japan's Nuclear Crisis Deepens, China Expresses 'Shock'*. Available at: www.reuters.com/article/2013/08/21/us-japan-fukushima-severity-idUSBRE97K02B20130821 (Accessed July 2015).

Taylor, Robert P, Chandrasekar Govindarajalu, Jeremy Levin, Anke S. Meyer, and William A. Ward (2008) *Financing Energy Efficiency: Lessons from Brazil, China, India, and Beyond*. Washington, DC: World Bank.

Trabish, Herman K. 2013. "FERC Chair Jon Wellinghoff: Solar 'Is Going to Overtake Everything.'" Greentech Media. August 21. Available at http://www.greentechmedia.com/articles/read/ferc-chair-wellinghoff-sees-a-solar-future-and-a-utility-of-the-future?utm_source=Daily&utm_medium=Headline&utm_campaign=GTMDaily.

Victor, Peter (2008) *Managing without Growth: Slower by Design, Not Disaster,* Northampton, MA: Edward Elgar.

World Bank (2015) World Development Indicators. Washington, DC. Available at: http://data.worldbank.org/indicator (Accessed July 2015).

Index

A
Alternative ownership forms, 99–104
Amsden, Alice, 99
Appliances
    rebound effect and, 41–42
Australia
    current emissions, 17
Automobiles, 13
    rebound effect and, 41

B
Baker, Mark, 51
Berkshire Hathaway, 120
Bioenergy, 45–47
    capital costs for expanding, estimates of, 58–61
    "carbon sink" effect, 47–48
    electricity generation using, 54, 60–61
    expansion of, problems with, 47–50
    food supply, effect on, 47–49
    India, in, 60–61
Bolinger, Mark, 100
Brazil
    assumptions underlying estimates on emissions reductions, 128–131
    current emissions, 16, 129–130

current energy consumption, 14–15

energy intensity ratio, 35–36, 44

Financing Energy Efficiency: Lessons from Brazil, China, India and Beyond, 97

job creation estimates, 76–81

pre-salt deposits in, 9

wire-charge mechanism, 98

Buffett, Warren, 120

Business-as-usual scenario, 1 et seq., 57–72, 114, 129–131

C

Canada

current emissions, 17

Carbon caps, 46, 57–58, 96

Carbon capture and sequestration, 19, 21, 25–27, 30

"Carbon sink" effect, 47–48

Carbon taxes, 46, 57–58, 96

Carbon Tracker, 9, 118

CCS. *See* Carbon capture and sequestration

China

assumptions underlying estimates on emissions reductions, 128–131

current energy consumption, 12–15

efficiency gains, 39

energy intensity ratio, 35–36

Financing Energy Efficiency: Lessons from Brazil, China, India and Beyond, 97

hydro power in, 50

job creation estimates, 76–81

loan guarantee programs, 97

reduction target and, 70, 72, 116–117

Three Gorges Dam, 50

Clean renewables. *See* Renewable energy

Climate stabilization, 3–4, 6, 9, 69, 90

CCS, effect of, 26

de-growth approach to, 20, 107–109

divestment movement, 120–121

employment, effect of investment on (*See* Job expansion)

energy conservation's role in, 32
energy efficiency investments as driving force, 114–115
global climate change, 111–116
global fairness as issue in, 14–15, 14–18, 116–118
insuring against climate change, investments as, 20, 111–116
issues, generally, 110–111
job losses from policies for, 6
political perspective, 119
resistance to, 4, 9, 90, 100, 118–121
risk assessment, 111 et seq.
Coal
carbon taxes and carbon caps, 57–58
CCS, effect of, 26
consumption levels, 4–5, 8–9, 22
divestment movement, 120–121
energy provided by one Q-BTU, 13
fuel switching, 21, 23–25
rebound effect per Jevons, 40–41, 43
Contamination
fracking, from, 23–24
nuclear energy, from, 28–30
Corn ethanol, 48
Current policies scenario, 10–11, 127
"Cursed" resources, fossil fuels as, 107

D
De-growth as solution to emissions problem, 20, 107–109
Divestment movement, 120–121

E
Edison Electric Institute, 102
Electricity
community ownership structures, effect of, 100–104
cost of producing, 6, 23, 53–55, 60–61, 101, 112, 122–123
energy provided by one Q-BTU, 13
feed-in tariffs, 96–97
Emanuel, Kerry, 1, 111, 113

Emissions, 1–3, 21–22
    bioenergy, from, 47–48
    Brazil, 16, 129–130
    carbon capture and sequestration, 19, 21, 25–27, 30
    "carbon sink" effect, 47–48
    current levels, 12–17
    de-growth as solution, 20, 107–109
    energy efficiency as best way to reduce (*See* Energy efficiency)
    fuel switching, effect of, 21, 23–25
    global fairness as issue in reducing, 14–18, 116–118
    low-income and high-income countries compared, 15–18
    nuclear power, from, 27–28
    per capita GDP, relationship to, 15–18
    projections for 2035, 10–12
    reduction target (*See* Reduction target)
Employment effects. *See* Job expansion
Energiewende, 130
Energy Concept document, 36, 130, 131
Energy conservation
    energy efficiency compared, 31–32
Energy consumption
    bioenergy, 45, 47
    country-by-country levels of, 12–15
    energy efficiency, reductions through, 34–36
    levels of, 12–15, 21–22
    operation of buildings, caused by, 36
    reduction target, effect of (*See* Reduction target)
Energy efficiency
    assumptions for individual country estimates on emissions
            reductions, 128–131
    clean energy investment program and IEA current policies scenario
            compared, 127–128
    complementary policies to reduce emissions, 43–44
    cost assumptions and capacity expansion, 127
    cost of achieving one Q-BTU gain in, 131
    critical policy tool, as, 33–36

employment, effect on (*See* Job expansion)
energy conservation compared, 31–32
energy intensity ratios, 35–36
improvements in, 39
investment, benefits of, 34–36, 38, 114–115
investment costs, 5, 37–39, 64
loan guarantee programs, 97–98
payback period for investments in, 39
rebound effects, 40–44
reduction target, role in (*See* Reduction target)
spending trajectory for investments, 125–126
upfront investment as hindrance, 39–40
Energy Efficiency Market Report, 97
Energy Information Agency, 23
capital costs as to renewable electricity capacity, 123 et seq.
emissions projections for 2035, 10–12
Fukushima meltdown, 29–30
Energy intensity ratios, 43–44
Environmental benefits from emissions reduction, 6–7
Environmental concerns, 26–28

F
Feed-in tariffs, 96–97
Financial Times, 102
Financing Energy Efficiency: Lessons from Brazil, China, India and Beyond, 97
Food supply and food prices, 47–50
Fossil fuels
carbon caps (*See* Carbon caps)
carbon taxes (*See* Carbon taxes)
consumption levels, 8–9, 21–22, 67, 105
"cursed" resources, as, 107
divestment movement, 120–121
electricity generation using, 54
employees in sector, assistance for displaced, 89–91
employment effect of consumption reduction, 72, 73, 74–75
fight against fossil fuel companies, 9, 90, 100, 118–121

fuel switching, 21, 23–25
imports and exports, 104–107
potential losses by asset owners, 9, 118–120
publicly-owned national companies, 99–103
reduction target, role in (*See* Reduction target)
renewable energy costs compared, 55–58
subsidies for, 46, 55–58, 115
transition to renewables, issues in, 9, 89–91, 104–107, 115–116
    450/Low-Carbon case, 10–11, 12
Fracking, 9, 23–24
France
emissions levels, 16
Fuel switching, 21, 23–25
Fukushima meltdown, 29–30

G
GDP
assumptions in twenty-year clean energy project, 5–6, 62–66, 114,
    116–118
de-growth scenario, effect of, 20, 108–109
low-income and high-income countries compared, 15–18
per capita emissions, relationship to, 15–18
GDP, scaling effects to 1.5% of, 5, 7–8, 65, 69, 80–83
Geothermal energy, 45–47 passim
electricity generation using, 54
Germany
assumptions underlying estimates on emissions reductions, 128–131
community-owned clean energy systems, 103–104
current energy consumption, 12, 14–15
efficiency gains, 39
emissions, 129–130
Energiewende, 130
Energy Concept document, 36, 130, 131
energy efficiency in, 35–36
energy intensity ratio, 35–36, 44
financing policies, 97

importation of energy, 105
job creation estimates, 76–81
Global fairness, 14–18, 116–118
Grantham Institute on Climate Change and the Environment, 9, 118
Green Jobs: Toward Decent Work in a Sustainable, Low-Carbon World, 89
Greenhouse gas emissions. *See* Emissions
Griffith-Jones, Stephanie, 98

H
Hydraulic fracturing technology. *See* Fracking
Hydro power, 45–47 *passim*
    capital costs for expanding, estimates of, 58–61
    India, in, 51
    large- and small-scale projects compared, 50–52

I
IEA. *See* International Energy Agency
Imports and exports, effect of transition to clean energy on, 104–107
India
    assumptions underlying estimates on emissions reductions, 128–131
    bioenergy in, 60–61
    current energy consumption, 12, 14–15
    energy efficiency in, 42
    energy intensity ratio, 35–36
    Financing Energy Efficiency: Lessons from Brazil, China, India and Beyond, 97
    hydro power in, 51
    job creation estimates, 76–81
    reduction target and, 70, 71, 116–117
    renewable energy costs in, 60–61
Indonesia
    assumptions underlying estimates on emissions reductions, 128–131
    current energy consumption, 12, 14–15
    energy intensity ratio, 35–36
    exportation of energy, 106–107
    job creation estimates, 76–81

reduction target and, 70, 71–72, 117–118

Integrated Energy Policy Report, 42

International Energy Agency, 55, 56, 57

    business-as-usual scenario (*See* Business-as-usual scenario)

    clean energy investment program and IEA current policies scenario
        compared, 127–128

    emissions projections for 2035, 10–12

    Energy Efficiency Market Report, 97

    reduction target, estimates as to (*See* Reduction target)

International Energy Outlook, 29–30

International Labour Office, 88

International Panel on Climate Change, 1, 4, 59, 69

    reduction target (*See* Reduction target)

International Renewable Energy Agency, 6, 46, 60, 61, 122–123

IPCC. *See* International Panel on Climate Change

IRENA. *See* International Renewable Energy Agency

Is War Necessary for Economic Growth?, 94

J

Jackson, Robert, 23

Jevons, William Stanley, 40–41

Job expansion, 4, 73–75

    country-specific estimates, 76–80

    data used in estimates, 75–76

    de-growth scenario, effect of, 20, 109

    domestic content of spending as factor in, 80

    economic sectors with large employment increases, 85–86

    education and skill requirements, 87–89

    fossil fuel producers and importers compared, 76–78, 79, 80–83

    fossil fuel sector employees, transition for, 9, 89–91

    GDP, scaling effects to 1.5% of, 7–8, 80–83

    improvement in job quality, 85–87

    informal employment sector, 86–87

    input-output tables, use of, 75–76

    labor intensity as factor in, 80

    labor productivity growth, 83–85

net job creation, 82–83
wage levels, differences caused by, 78
women, opportunities for, 87

K
Keystone pipeline project, 74
Koch brothers, 119, 121

L
Li, Liwan, 103
London School of Economics, 9, 118
Low-Carbon case, 10–11, 12
Low-Cost Technology case, 123

M
Mazzucato, Mariana, 95
Mazzzocchi, Tony, 90
McKinsey study, 33–34, 37, 38
Mobilizing Investment for Inclusive Green Growth in Low-Income Countries, 98
Model for estimating reductions via investment program, 125–131

N
National Academy of Sciences, 34
National development banks, 97–99
Natural gas
   carbon caps (*See* Carbon caps)
   carbon taxes (*See* Carbon taxes)
   consumption levels, 4–5, 8–9, 22
   fuel switching, 21, 23–25
   publicly-owned national companies, 99–103
New Development Bank, 98
New Policies case, 11
Nuclear meltdowns, 28–30
Nuclear power, 27–30, 65, 112

O

Ocampo, Jose Antonio, 98

Oil

    carbon caps (*See* Carbon caps)

    carbon taxes (*See* Carbon taxes)

    consumption levels, 4–5, 8–9, 22

    divestment movement, 120–121

    publicly-owned national companies, 99–103

P

Policy framework, 92–93

    alternative ownership forms, 99–103

    carbon caps (*See* Carbon caps)

    carbon taxes (*See* Carbon taxes)

    community-owned clean energy systems, 103–104

    de-growth as solution to emissions problem, 20, 107–109

    effective industrial policies, 93–95

    feed-in tariffs, 96–97

    financing policies, 97–99

    free market perspective, 94–95

    imports and exports, 104–107

    large and stable clean energy markets, creation of, 95–97

    large-scale government investment, need for, 95–97

Power plant decommissioning, 28

Public health benefits from emissions reduction, 6–7

Public ownership of national energy companies, 99–103

R

Radioactive waste, 28

Real Prospects for Energy Efficiency in the United States, 34–35

Rebound effects, 40–44

Reduction target, 3–5, 8–9, 15–20, 18–20

    assumptions for individual country estimates on emissions

        reductions, 128–131

    business-as-usual scenario, 57–72, 114

    cost of achieving, 59–60

country-specific reductions, 70–72
energy efficiency, increase in, 65 et seq.
environmental benefits from emissions reduction, 6–7
ethical issues, 117–118
fossil fuel energy consumption, 65, 66, 67, 69
GDP assumptions, 62–66
global emissions, decrease in, 65 et seq., 70
global energy consumption, fall in, 65 et seq.
global fairness as issue in, 14–18, 116–118
Indonesia, 117–118
model for estimating reductions via investment program, 125–131
national development banks, role of, 97–99
per capita emissions, 15–18, 69, 70
policies to achieve (*See* Policy framework)
public health benefits from reduction, 6–7
renewables, increase in, 65 et seq.
resistance by fossil fuel companies, 4, 9, 90, 100, 118–121
total emissions, 65, 68
twenty-year program and BAU scenario compared, 65, 69
Reference case, 10–12
Renewable energy, 5–6
capital costs, 5–6, 58–61, 124
capital costs as to renewable electricity capacity, 123 et seq.
clean energy investment program and IEA current policies scenario
 compared, 127–128
cost assumptions and capacity expansion, 127
costs of generating, 46–47, 53–61
current levels of consumption, 45–46
current levels of investment, 7–8
distributed energy supply systems powered by, 102
employment, effect of investment on (*See* Job expansion)
expansion, costs of, 58–61, 64, 122–123, 127
fossil fuel costs compared, 55–58
GDP, scaling effects to 1.5% of, 5, 7–8, 65, 69, 80–83
hydro power (*See* Hydro power)
imports and exports, effect of transition on, 104–107

India, costs in, 60–61
industrial policies as to clean energy economies, 93–95
insuring against climate change, investing as, 20, 111–116
intermittency as factor in, 52
investment's role in climate stabilization, 114–115
Low-Cost Technology case, 123
model for estimating reductions via investment program, 125–131
reduction target, role in (*See* Reduction target)
solar power (*See* Solar power)
wind power (*See* Wind power)
Risk assessment, 111 et seq.
nuclear power, from, 27–30
Romm, Joseph, 25–26
Ruttan, Vernon, 94

S
Sarkar, Ashok, 33
Singh, Jas, 33
Skills for Green Jobs: a Global View, 88
Solar energy, 45–47 passim
alternative ownership structures and, 102–103
capital costs for expanding, estimates of, 58–61
cost of, 54–55
distributed energy supply systems powered by, 102
electricity generation using, 6, 54–55
intermittency as factor in, 52
Solomon, Ezra, 62
South Africa, 70–71
assumptions underlying estimates on emissions reductions, 128–131
current energy consumption, 12, 14–15
energy intensity ratio, 35–36, 44
job creation estimates, 76–81
South Korea
assumptions underlying estimates on emissions reductions, 128–131
current energy consumption, 12, 14–15
energy intensity ratio, 35–36, 44

importation of energy, 105
job creation estimates, 76–81
Spain, 70–71
assumptions underlying estimates on emissions reductions, 128–131
current energy consumption, 14–15
energy intensity ratio, 35–36
importation of energy, 105
job creation estimates, 76–81
Spratt, Stephen, 98
Storage of spent reactor fuel, 28
Sub-Saharan Africa
exportation of energy, 107
Subsidies for fossil fuels, 46, 55–58, 115
Superfund for workers, 90
Sustainable Energy in America Factbook, 55
Sweden
emissions levels, 16
Switzerland
emissions levels, 16

T
The Coal Question, 40–41
The Entrepreneurial State, 95
The Rise of "The Rest," 99
Three Gorges Dam, 50
Twenty-year clean energy investment project, 4–6, 62–72, 73–74, 116, 124
model for estimating reductions via investment program, 125–131

U
UNEP. *See* United Nations Environmental Program
United Nations Environmental Program, 89
United States
assumptions underlying estimates on emissions reductions, 128–131
current emissions, 16, 18

current energy consumption, 12–15
energy intensity ratio, 35–36, 44
energy provided by one Q-BTU, 13
job creation estimates, 76–81
reduction target and, 18, 116–117

W
Wellinghoff, Jon, 55
What We Know About Climate Change, 1
Wind power, 45–47 passim
    capital costs for expanding, estimates of, 58–61
    community ownership structures, 100–102
    distributed energy supply systems powered by, 102
    electricity generation using, 54
    intermittency as factor in, 52
Wire-charge mechanism, 98
World Bank studies, 15, 33, 37–38, 97
    hydro power, 51, 61
World Energy Outlook, 10
    CCS, view of, 27

Acknowledgments

This is a small book, but it has emerged out of a wide range of work I have done in collaboration with a large number of organizations and people over the past seven years. The overarching goal with all of these endeavors has been simple and yet daunting: to figure out how to build a global green economy within the next twenty years that can succeed both in stabilizing the climate and expanding human well-being. It is a great pleasure to now recognize many of the organizations and people with whom I have worked on these massively challenging issues.

I begin with the many organizations who commissioned me, along with my coworkers at the Political Economy Research Institute (PERI), to conduct studies on various aspects of building a green economy, controlling climate change and expanding good job opportunities, in the United States and globally. These include the Arca Foundation, the Blue/Green Alliance, the Ford Foundation, the International Labour Organization, Green for All, the Labor Network for Sustainability, the Natural Resources Defense Council, Podemos, the Surdna Foundation, the U.S. Department of Energy, and the World Wildlife Federation of Canada.

Three organizations commissioned me to produce the book-length research volumes that constitute a good share of the backbone of this book. The first two are the Global Green Growth Institute (GGGI) in Seoul and the United Nations Industrial Development Organization (UNIDO), which jointly published our study *Global Green Growth: Clean Energy Industrial Investments and Expanding Job Opportunities* in June 2015. I want to thank Myung Kyoon Lee and De Yeon Choi of GGGI and especially Ascha Lychett Pedersen of UNIDO for their constructive efforts and professionalism on this project.

The other organization is the Center for American Progress (CAP) in Washington, D.C. My work with CAP began in 2008, and led to the publication of *Green Recovery* in 2008, *The Economic Benefits of Investing in Clean Energy* in 2009 and finally, in 2014, *Green Growth: A U.S. Program for Controlling Climate Change and Expanding Job Opportunities*. I received tremendous support from Danielle Baussan and Ben Bovarnick, and from former CAP staffers Mike Ettlinger and Adam James at different stages in these projects. Bracken Hendricks was my closest collaborator at CAP throughout this full six-year stretch of work. Bracken was relentless in his efforts to get things right, including as a co-author on *Green Growth*. That made it much harder for me to get things wrong.

My other coauthors were Heidi Garrett-Peltier and James Heintz of PERI on *Green Growth*, and Shouvik Chakraborty, along with Heidi and James on *Global Green Growth*. They all brought original thinking, hard work, and team spirit to both projects. Heidi has also done brilliant research for years in developing a workable methodology for measuring how clean energy investments create jobs throughout the world. Ying Chen also made important contributions, including in her forthcoming

Ph.D. dissertation, which enabled us to apply this job estima-
tion methodology for the critical case of China.

All of this work emerged out of the high-spirited community
within the Department of Economics of the University of Massachusetts–Amherst and PERI. I can't imagine a better place to
be situated for trying to make some progress as an economics
teacher and researcher toward advancing human and ecological
well-being. My dedication of this book to three members of this
community, Judy Fogg, Jerry Epstein, and Jim Boyce, is meant
to also reflect my broader appreciation and respect for everyone
contributing to the vibrancy and sense of purpose within UMass
Economics and PERI.

I am extremely fortunate to have again worked with MIT
Press and *Boston Review* on this book. Deb Chasman, coeditor of
Boston Review, has been, as always, equally outstanding as a big
thinker, hard-nosed editor, and friend. Deb's editing associate
Matt Lord made many valuable suggestions that improved the
book. The idea for the book emerged through discussions with
Clay Morgan, who had been the Environmental Sciences editor
at MIT Press until his recent retirement. I also greatly appreciate
the support of Clay's successor Beth Clevenger and her assistant
Miranda Martin, as well as Marc Lowenthal and Colleen Lanick
at MIT. Working as independent consultants, Kim Weinstein did
a beautiful job with the layout of the book, working under a
ridiculously tight deadline; and James Connell did an outstanding job with the index.

I rely on the love and support of my mother, Irene Pollin,
and draw inspiration from the memory of my father, Abe Pollin. Hannah and Asaf Pollin-Galay are so wonderfully engaged
in their own creative projects that my efforts receive steady
booster injections through osmosis alone. My granddaughter

Ruthie Pollin-Galay wrote at least twenty books just over the past year in kindergarten alone, and hers include great drawings as well as words. This one picture-less volume represents my feeble attempt to keep up. Sigrid Miller Pollin knows, literally from the ground up, about creating a green economy, having designed and supervised construction over the past several years of multiple buildings that are green, functional, and beautiful. From having been together for forty years, I have by now figured out that I probably won't go too far wrong by following her example.

About the Author

Robert Pollin is Distinguished Professor of Economics and Co-Director of the Political Economy Research Institute (PERI) at the University of Massachusetts-Amherst. He is also the founder and President of PEAR (Pollin Energy and Retrofits), an Amherst, MA–based green energy company operating throughout the United States. His books include *The Living Wage: Building a Fair Economy* (coauthored 1998); *Contours of Descent: U.S. Economic Fractures and the Landscape of Global Austerity* (2003); *An Employment-Targeted Economic Program for South Africa* (co-authored 2007); *A Measure of Fairness: The Economics of Living Wages and Minimum Wages in the United States* (co-authored 2008), *Back to Full Employment* (2012), *Green Growth* (2014), and *Global Green Growth* (2015). He has worked recently as a consultant for the U.S. Department of Energy, the International Labour Organization, the United Nations Industrial Development Organization and numerous non-governmental organizations in several countries on various aspects of building high-employment green economies. He has also directed projects on employment creation and poverty reduction in sub-Saharan Africa for the United Nations Development Program, and has worked with many U.S. non-governmental organizations on creating living wage statutes at both the statewide and municipal levels. He is presently a member of the Scientific Advisory Committee of the European Commission project on Financialization, Economy, Society, and Sustainable Development (FESSUD). He was selected by *Foreign Policy* magazine as one of the "100 Leading Global Thinkers for 2013."